Laura Demasi is a Sydney-based writer. She has written for national publications including *Vogue*, *Elle* and the *Sydney Morning Herald*. *The Ladies' Room* is her first book.

LAURA DEMASI

the ladies' room

HarperCollinsPublishers

HarperCollins*Publishers*

First published in Australia in 2002
by HarperCollins*Publishers* Pty Limited
ABN 36 009 913 517
A member of the HarperCollins*Publishers* (Australia) Pty Limited Group
www.harpercollins.com.au

HarperCollins*Publishers*
25 Ryde Road, Pymble, Sydney NSW 2073, Australia
31 View Road, Glenfield, Auckland 10, New Zealand
77–85 Fulham Palace Road, London W6 8JB, United Kingdom
Hazelton Lanes, 55 Avenue Road, Suite 2900, Toronto, Ontario, M5R 3L2
and 1995 Markham Road, Scarborough, Ontario, M1B 5M8, Canada
10 East 53rd Street, New York NY 10022, USA

National Library of Australia Cataloguing-in-publication data:

Demasi, Laura.
The ladies' room.
ISBN 0 7322 7487 7.
I. Title.
A823.3

Cover photograph: Getty Images
Author photograph: Josh Evans
Cover design: Katie Mitchell, HarperCollins Design Studio
Internal design: Christa Edmonds, HarperCollins Design Studio
Typeset in 11.5 on 16 Minion by HarperCollins Design Studio
Printed and bound in Australia by Griffin Press on 80gsm Econoprint

5 4 3 2 1 02 03 04 05

For Maria Demasi and Josh Evans

introduction

Welcome to *The Ladies' Room*. Consider this your 'access all areas' pass to the intimate thoughts of some of Australia's most fascinating women.

The Ladies' Room is a chronicle of the conversations I have had over the past year with some of the women I admire. Most have racked up a list of firsts as a woman or a professional, some are ground breakers, some are interesting thinkers, some are prolific story tellers, some are adventurers.

What a journey it has been. Some of those conversations were epics that stretched from breakfast to lunch, from lunch to dinner and late into the night. The kind that leave you feeling as if you've been on a long train journey, enriched by what you've seen and heard, but exhausted by having had so much to take in that you need a night's sleep to recover. Then there were others — the fast and the furious, a rapid fire of stories, thoughts and ideas articulated with such vigour that you are left standing in awe. Like watching a firecracker's unstoppable trajectory, spurting beams of light in every direction, before the fading sparks commence their descent back to down to earth.

I hope you will view these stories not just as a window into the lives of these particular women, but as a chronicle of sorts, a portrait of a generation of women, and intimate snapshots of what it is like to be a successful woman in 2002.

I hope you are entertained, inspired and occasionally enlightened by their honest and candid accounts of their adventures through life — from Kirsty Sword Gusmao's life-threatening role as a double agent in the East Timorese Resistance movement (and one of the most extraordinary love stories *ever*), to Lee Tulloch's amusing account of watching rich socialites disappear into their absurdly voluminous Christian Lacroix *pouf* skirts at the famous New York restaurant Le Cirque.

Or the pioneering and inspiring endeavours of conductor Simone Young and theatre director Gale Edwards, who many times over have the been the first women, and often the first Australians to conduct and direct for the greatest artistic companies around the world — from *Lohengrin* at the Vienna Staatsoper to *Jesus Christ Superstar* on the West End and Broadway.

On a more personal level, I hope you find a sense of solidarity and understanding in the accounts of what success costs a woman these days. How success sometimes comes back to bite you, how you can be feted one day and discarded the next, and just how tough, wearying and consuming it can all be sometimes.

So sit back, take a moment and have a peek into the lives of some of some amazing women — who knows where it will lead …

I hope you enjoy your stay in the *Ladies' Room.*

Laura Demasi
June 2002

contents

introduction	vii
collette dinnigan	1
donna hay	23
elizabeth macgregor	43
gale edwards	67
jan chapman	99
kirsty sword gusmao	117
lee tulloch	149
libbi gorr	179
liz broderick	197
marion hume	215
rachel perkins	245
simone young	275
acknowledgments	305

collette dinnigan

collette dinnigan

When Collette Dinnigan first took a suitcase full of her lacy dresses to Paris, the concept of Australian fashion, if indeed one existed beyond these shores then, was limited to board shorts, loud shirts and Akubras. But after Dinnigan hit town, word spread that Australia could produce something original and artfully made, and in Dinnigan's case, capable of competing against the stars of the international fashion world.

In 1995 Dinnigan became the first Australian-based designer to mount a full-scale ready-to-wear show at the Paris collections, an invitation-only event for designers. Dinnigan's delicious take on soft, feminine dressing was a hit and her label was picked up by stores all around the world.

Finally, Australian fashion had a face and a profile, and Dinnigan's success paved the way for a whole new generation of Australian-based designers who started thinking globally for the first time.

But Dinnigan's story is not just about pretty dresses. Recognised as much for her business sense as she is for her expertise as a designer, Dinnigan has been the recipient of numerous awards. In 1998 she was inducted into the Australian Businesswomen's Hall of Fame and has served as Chairperson of The New South Wales Small Business Development Corporation. She is also still the only Australian-based designer invited to show in the official schedule of the Paris collections.

I first came to Australia from New Zealand when I was 19. I travelled quite a lot with my family when I was young. I was born in South Africa and when I was eight years old we sailed all the way from there to New Zealand. So it wasn't a big deal for me to travel to Australia alone. I was very independent. I was brought up in a wonderful family of strong, determined characters and we were all independent in our own way. I think that independence gave me the confidence to take things on. Not necessarily confidence in myself — I was actually very shy and I found that quite difficult — but more in the idea of doing something important and interesting with my life.

I came to Australia because there wasn't a lot of work for me in New Zealand. It was still a very small country when I left in 1985 and there wasn't a lot happening in fashion. I did a fashion and textiles course in Wellington and I actually wanted to work in film and TV costume design initially but the market for that in New Zealand was even smaller. There was definitely a lot more on offer in Australia.

I'm certainly not the first person to leave a small place in search of opportunity. It's a very New Zealander thing to do, and I take my hat off to New Zealanders for it. They are very courageous people and they'll travel the world to realise their ambitions. They are a lot like the people who live in the smaller countries in and around Europe, like Belgium. Not all things are on your doorstep so you have to work a bit harder than other people, and sometimes you have to fight for it. That's why it's so precious when you do achieve some success — but then things are never quite as enticing when you're handed them on a platter.

Australians are the same really. I think some of the more ambitious Australians see Australia as a kind of backyard testing ground, and I agree to a certain extent. We are isolated from the rest of the world so you can experiment with things here. But then once you get it right you can use the rest of the world as a stage and go for it.

I think a good dose of naivety helps. It certainly worked in my favour. If I had known the hardships and obstacles involved in the path I was going to take, it wouldn't have been anywhere near as attractive. It's definitely better not to contemplate the possible downside of things too much, otherwise you'd never try anything.

Taking your product to the rest of the world forces you to become a great salesperson. You're always having to convince everybody of how fantastic it is because you're on the back foot to start with. You don't have a reputation, you don't have any contacts, not in the beginning anyway, so it's really just your enthusiasm and the quality of your work that will get you noticed. You've got to have a lot of energy when you first start out, because believe me, you really need it if you're determined to make things work.

That first move to Sydney was great for me. Thank God I did it. There was so much more opportunity here. I got a job in the ABC TV costume department, which I loved, but it was hard for the first few years. I didn't have a history with anyone here. I had none of the usual ties that give your life a sense of foundation and grounding — I had no family, no old school buddies or friends from childhood, so I was really on my own. I do have some very good friends here now after all those years, but not a lot. Just a few close friends.

I consider Australia my home now, but New Zealand has become more and more appealing to me. It's ironic because the things I love about New Zealand now are the very same things I didn't like about it when I lived there, and the reason I left in the first place. Now I love the fact that it's so far away from everything and there are hardly any people around, and everyone is so laid-back. It's not a fast place but it's very genuine.

New Zealand is very different to Australia. Sydney, in particular, is the land of opportunity. It's a place where you can make fast money, if that's what you want. It's almost like Los Angeles now in some ways. There's an insincerity in Sydney you don't see in other cities in Australia, like Melbourne. Like any big city, there is a part of Sydney society that can be shallow. There's also not a lot of re-investing in people and talent. Once you've had a measure of success people tend to lose interest, they're already out there looking for the next big thing. I guess that comes from the transitory nature of big city life — people do come and go a lot more.

But saying that, there is a wonderful intellectual side to Sydney, which is quite motivating. It's up to you to choose which world you want to be part of. I've met people here who I have a tremendous amount of respect for, people whose minds I appreciate enormously, and some of them have become mentors to me. I think you discover where you fit into the world as you get older; you become a bit wiser and learn how to take the good things from a place and turn a blind eye to the rest.

Essentially, I think Sydney is like any big, fast city. It is dynamic and innovative and the rest is what you make of it. You just have to balance the fastness of it all with other things. And you've always got to keep a check of yourself, because the reality is, you come into this world alone and leave it alone. Just enjoy it and be good to people along the way.

While I was working in costume design I started making lingerie as gifts for friends. I've always loved lingerie and there was virtually nothing being made in Australia. Some of the magazine editors in Sydney had seen pieces through people I knew and they started putting in orders for themselves. My lingerie business, which is how it originally started, just grew from there. I started to sell to Barneys in New York and Harvey Nichols in London but it was really difficult to sell to stores here. Mind you, getting into Barneys wasn't exactly easy. I remember faxing them some of the press I'd received in magazines. I faxed so many times and no one ever returned my calls when I rang to follow them up. It turns out that I was faxing the doorman instead of the buying office! Apparently, he quite enjoyed all the pictures of girls in lingerie. When I finally did get in contact with the buying office, they loved the collection. I flew to New York to show them samples and they picked me up. They really understood what I was trying to do, whereas buyers in Australia weren't interested, either because they thought it was too expensive or because they believed people only shopped for lingerie at department stores. Of course, getting into the department stores in Australia was near impossible. They weren't interested in new talent like the American stores were, and I wasn't a well-known label at that stage.

There was nothing I could do about it. I couldn't move forward, no matter what I tried. I found the tunnel vision of some people so aggravating, but it was the mid-1980s I guess, when everything was so label orientated. It was all about big fashion houses and flashy marketing campaigns, not new talent.

Out of frustration I made the decision to open my own shop in Paddington, about 11 years ago now. Initially it was very difficult to raise capital, the banks weren't very interested in lending to young women then. I remember one bank manager telling me quite blatantly, 'You're in your early twenties. What happens if you get pregnant and have a baby? The business will collapse and we'll lose our money.'

The banks did lose a lot of money in the 1980s and 1990s and there were so many scandals, so I assume that kind of attitude was just a by-product of it all, but I couldn't help feeling as though I was getting a raw deal. It made things very hard because there are times when you need finance to stay alive. But in retrospect, I think those difficulties act as a sifting process in life. Things need to be a bit hard, because if they aren't, too many people would be doing it.

In any case, I was lucky because my shop did very well. My customers kept coming back and after a while they started asking me to make them things like pyjamas and evening pants. They started wearing my silk slips as dresses and my corsets as evening wear. It was a very pretty, feminine, sensual way of dressing and after a decade of wearing structured suits, I think that's what women wanted. It was part of the whole lingerie as outer wear movement.

The big international fashion magazines like American *Harper's Bazaar* and British *Vogue* credited the label as being part of starting that movement, which gave us great credibility. It was quite an achievement to be recognised for something on that level when we were still a relatively small operation based in Australia. There was no such thing as Australian Fashion Week then; the only international exposure you got was what you generated yourself.

Once I opened my own store and started making dresses everything just kept growing from there. I started selling overseas a lot more. I would go on regular selling trips to Hong Kong, London, New York and Los Angeles. Those really long trips became quite tedious after a while, and it was actually one of the buyers I knew, Mary Gallagher from Harvey Nichols, who suggested I show in Paris during the collections when all the buyers were in town at once. It made more sense to do it that way, it was much easier to travel to one city rather than four.

The next season I showed in Paris for the first time, in a friend's house. I had a few samples hanging on a rack in his living room and I took appointments with buyers, who came through word of mouth. In the end all of the buyers came. They kept saying, 'Why don't you do a show? Nobody understands how to wear your corsets and lace slips.' So the next season, in October 1995, I did.

I was aware that no Australian designer had ever shown in Paris before, but I didn't feel as though I was doing anything particularly special at the time. In fact, I wish somebody had done it before me, I really could have used their help. To begin with, I had no idea there was such a thing as the Chambre Syndicale, the body which organises the collections in Paris each season. Of course, nor did I know that there was an official calendar of shows and to participate you had to be invited. It seems unbelievable now but I didn't have a clue. Even fashion students know all about this kind of thing now. I did two shows in Paris off the official calendar and each time I invited members of the Chambre Syndicale and continued to send them press and information on the collections in-between. Eventually, my label came before the Chambre Syndicale's board and they decided to invite me into the official calendar. It was very difficult, and it still is. I'm still the only Australian-based designer on the official schedule in Paris.

People think it's great to be the first person to do something because you go down in history, and it is true, you do feel a certain sense of achievement. But I never started out with a grand plan to become a public person. I had a craft and I wanted to better it, and yes, I did want to take it to the world and I was very determined and focused about it, but it was never my intention to be the first Australian designer to show in Paris. That just kind of happened. It did change my life, however.

It's actually very difficult being a leader because there's no bench-mark. Everything is a new experience; everything you do is totally from scratch and it costs a lot of money to learn. Being a pioneer in an industry really does have its pitfalls. The more determined you are to make a mark, the more hurdles you have to cross.

On that first trip to Paris, I remember ringing the embassies for help. I had none of the right contacts and no one knew who I was, so of course they never returned my phone calls. It's a very different story now but back then it was just so hard. In the end, after trying in vain to get some help I decided it would be easier if I did everything myself. It was quite an horrific time in Paris as well, with all of the problems with the Algerian terrorist bombings in the subway, and the transport strikes. If I'd known how hard it was going to be then I don't think I would have attempted it.

Economically it was difficult as well because the value of the Australian dollar was so low. Travelling overseas was always very expensive, and taking a whole collection over made it even worse. Getting around Paris was difficult because I didn't speak the language and I didn't have basic contacts. I didn't even know where to start looking for something as simple as a hairdresser.

I made my way around Paris on a friend's bicycle, riding around all day picking up things for the show, trying to find wigs for the models. Actually, aside from all the struggle, those were the fun days. My first show is still one of my favourites, even though I was so exhausted afterwards I couldn't move. Things are a lot more organised now, but there's still that anxiety you feel before a show. It's actually very frightening and it doesn't necessarily diminish as you get older. It's quite annoying in a way, you hope to grow out of those things. You're always wondering if you still have the edge, if you're still good enough. You never really know who your critic is: is it the customer, is it the press, or the advertising sector? Or is it your staff or your friends?

It's very different for young designers now. They are so focused on getting to a particular place that they don't think about the trail very much. Everything I did in those days was about trying to get my clothes out there, it was never about the final destination. It was never, 'I have to show in Paris' or 'I have to have this or that celebrity wearing my clothes'.

The whole culture of fashion design has changed. Now when you go to fashion school you can employ a sewer to make up your designs, rather than have to sew them yourself. It's very different from when I was studying; we were judged on how we sewed and constructed our designs. There was more of an emphasis on the craft of making clothes. It seems a lot easier now but having said that, it also seems to be a lot more competitive, probably because there are so many young designers out there.

When I started my business it seemed that Australians weren't interested in new talent or designers who had their own signature. Plagiarism was okay. It's only recently that Australian designers have started to judge themselves by international standards and the world has taken great interest in what is happening here.

The Australian fashion industry has progressed enormously now. Young designers are much more geared towards entering the global market. They're a lot more savvy, particularly with the media. They know how to build up their profiles. They set themselves specific goals: to be stocked in this or that store; to be in this or that magazine; to do a solo show at Australian Fashion Week by this time; and New York by this time; and all before they've produced their first collections. I think a lot of people try to launch themselves into the limelight rather than their product. It's very different to the organic way things evolved when I started. I imagine the pressure would be unbearable for a young designer now.

When I first began showing in Paris, Australian designers didn't have a presence in the international market so none of the newspapers sent journalists over to cover the shows. They did come eventually, writers like Melissa Hoyer from the *Sunday Telegraph* and Jane de Teliga, who was with the *Sydney Morning Herald* then. It's very nice because a lot of them credit their first trips to Paris and reporting on fashion as they do now because of me. I guess there was no reason for them to travel to Paris before then because there were no Australians to report on.

Those reports weren't run as fashion stories but as news stories, probably because of the newness and novelty of it all. I think newspaper editors realised people were quite interested in fashion and it wasn't just women and housewives either. Men were also interested in fashion, I think they enjoy the diversion of it all. That's changed the way Australia reported on fashion, which is interesting. A lot of the journalists go to the shows now because it's part of their job to report on what Australians are doing overseas.

So much has changed since I first started showing in Paris. Not just in the way Australians understand fashion, but in the way people around the world view Australia. When I first started doing business overseas the popular image of Australia was so incredibly different to what it is now, which is interesting because it wasn't all that long ago. I think people forget just how recent this image of Australia as a sophisticated and innovative place really is. When I first started going on selling trips to America people were still at the stage where they confused Australia with Austria or some other part of Europe. It sounds unbelievable, but it's true.

In Paris you'd try to tell the French about Australian wines or Australian food but they wouldn't take you seriously. Europeans didn't think there was any culture in Australia at all. Of course, now everyone recognises how wonderful Australian culture is, but back then no one believed we could make wine or cook as well as they did, or make films or music as great as theirs. That attitude was especially prevalent when it came to fashion. People in Paris found the very concept of Australian fashion ridiculous. They were entertained and amused by what you would consider it to be.

Because of this negative attitude, I made a conscious effort in Paris to introduce people to Australian food and wine. I remember one particular party I had there. Neil Perry, who's a friend, was in town so he did the cooking. He served really Australian dishes like scallops and had a particular species of wild boar from New South Wales specially sent over and we served Petaluma Riesling. Everybody loved it. They were quite astounded that our food was so sophisticated and tasted so good. They still talk about that party.

Of course, there's been quite a turnaround since then. It really is Australia's time now. Everyone talks about how good Australian food and wine is. And the fashion and the films. The actors and musicians. The beaches, the lifestyle. I think there are certain people we have to thank for that, people who raised the profile of Australia by venturing out into the world. You had Baz Luhrmann and Catherine Martin making movies like *Strictly Ballroom* and then *Romeo + Juliet*. Kylie Minogue doing so well in the UK, and Elle Macpherson, Sarah O'Hare and Nicole Kidman doing great things all over the world. Then Cate Blanchett came along and took the world by storm in *Elizabeth*. There are so many more. It was really wonderful to be part of that movement.

We're all quite consciously nationalistic. You do stick together in a way and support each other. There is this kind of pride we share, which is fantastic. You don't really find it in Australia, it's a special camaraderie that develops amongst Australians living or working outside the country. You're very supportive of each other's work and you want your friends to succeed, even more than if you were all living here.

A lot of us started together. I first met Catherine and Baz just after they finished *Strictly Ballroom*. We were living parallel lives: we were starting to do things overseas, we started young and went through our fair share of struggle. It was encouraging to be around people who were on a similar path. You could share your frustration with each other because you came across similar obstacles, even if they were in different areas you still understood what it was like. You didn't feel like you were alone with your problems.

Things started to happen for us at the same time. We

were able to buy our first houses around the same time, we became successful together. It didn't feel as though you left half of your friends behind. I think what we shared most was that we were very focused and hard-working. And full of fantasies, of course.

It's nice to share your success with the people who encouraged and supported you. I'm still very close to Catherine and Baz. I'm very proud of them. Obviously we do our own things as individuals, but collectively I think we've developed something distinctively Australian — a trademark, if you like.

It's been quite a journey up to this point in my life. Aside from all the creative and personal experiences, I have learnt an incredible amount about business. I still run every aspect of my business. I learnt most of what I know now along the way, it's been one big continuous learning curve. Having a lot of common sense helps and I've always been quite grounded. I'm not airy fairy and all over the place, I'm good at practical things.

It's so important to learn how to deal with all of the aspects of your business, rather than hand the tricky parts over to other people to deal with. That knowledge is quite empowering. It gives you control over your own destiny. You have to be involved in administering the business side of things if you want to take it to the next level. It's not just about making pretty dresses, it's a real business and it needs to be handled as such.

Understanding the business of fashion puts you on a different wavelength and it introduces you to a totally different circle of people. I've met some very interesting business people who have helped me a lot by sharing their knowledge. I'm the type of person who needs to be constantly stimulated and I enjoy meeting interesting people who have more knowledge than I do — you can learn so much from them. I don't think you can ever learn enough. Just when you think you've got everything right, you open up a whole new can of worms you knew nothing about.

Most people have an image of what it's like to be a designer based on what they read in magazines or newspapers, or whatever. Yes, it is exciting and you do get to travel around the world and meet some great people but the workload is unforgiving sometimes. People just don't understand the 20-hour days, or the times when you don't see the outside world for two weeks because the only time you leave the studio is for a couple of hours' sleep. And even when you are away from the studio, you're thinking about the business constantly.

Trying to run an international business from Australia is crazy sometimes. It is hard work and certainly hasn't made my life any easier. We do everything from here — the design, all the manufacturing. You don't have the resources here that you do in a place like Paris or New York. Instead of a choice between 100 buttons, you have a choice between two, and the two you can choose from are very expensive.

From a design point of view, being isolated from the rest of the fashion world does create a space in which you can be more original. Having said that, we're certainly not as isolated from the international industry as we used to be and so much of what's made here is plagiarised. I can't quite get my head around why a designer would want to do that. Obviously, some other people don't feel the same as I do about it. I think it's nice to be removed from the rest of the world sometimes. It is for me anyway because whenever I go away it's so intense. It's never a laid-back trip. Nothing is ever as intense as working and travelling at the same time.

Even after what I've achieved, I still have to work very hard to keep everything going. The business is a hungry machine that needs constant feeding. There's so much to do every day and it's hard work getting everything right. When you make mistakes you put systems in place so they don't happen again, but sometimes they do and then new mistakes in other parts of the business crop up.

Then you have to balance the running of the business with the creative side. The day-to-day running of things takes up so much time and head space that it does put a lot of pressure on your ability to be creative. It can be quite distressing when you feel like you can't create something, or that you've lost it. It's agonising and you can lose your confidence.

That's what I mean about the sifting process I mentioned earlier. There's so much involved in doing your own thing and it's so difficult that only a few people manage to outlast the struggle and rise to the top. You need a huge amount of focus and drive to work so hard. It's no use sitting back and waiting for opportunities to come to you; you need to create them, and take risks knowing that you will win some but also that you are going to lose others, and the ones you do lose you have to turn around. You can't procrastinate, or wait for the right timing because there isn't such a thing.

I have sacrificed a lot to get to where I am, but I'm at the stage now where I'm more conscious of not letting life pass me by. It's very easy for your work to infiltrate every area of your life: your social life, your personal and your family life. Even though I find what I do enormously fulfilling, it is important to have experiences that are totally separate from work.

I know I've missed a few goals I've kicked in my personal life because I worked so hard. But I started so young that I don't think I really knew any different. I had a very different twenties to most people. I created this label when I was 20 and I spent the rest of that decade trying to build it up. Then it took off in my thirties at a time when most people are only just starting to think seriously about their careers.

I've thought a lot about what it's taken to get me here

and I realise that there are parts of my life that need to slow down and other parts that need to speed up. I'm a very motivated person, so I could never wind down too much, and as much as I dream of doing nothing sometimes, I could never do it. I think I'll always be a bull at the gate; if I believe in something I just do it. And I rush at it. It's an instinctive reaction.

I did get divorced in the whole process but I don't think it's because I worked too hard. I think you always make time for the partner in your life no matter how hard you're working. Well, I did anyway. I got married quite young, when I was 24. It was a long relationship, 11 years, and it was great for a lot of that time. Marriage is not an institution.

You just know when a relationship changes. It's an instinctive thing, a gut feeling. You might try to kid or convince yourself it's just a phase and try to make it work but then it gets to the point where it becomes quite destructive. So you have to make the decision to move on and to do it as amicably as possible. If not, it's a shame because you erode the respect you have for each other.

I think anything in life that doesn't work out is disappointing because you put so much energy into it. You never go into something, especially a marriage, thinking it's not going to work so when it does break down it's incredibly sad. It's emotional, totally consuming and absorbing. With hindsight, it's easy to say, 'I should have done this or that,' but at the time you didn't and you can't change that. That's just one of the wonders of life: you never know how things are going to pan out.

The most important things in a relationship are that you trust and respect each other. And for me, I need to be with somebody I can bounce off. It's an interesting subject, I talk about it with my girlfriends quite often. I think there's a perception out there that men don't like strong women, either because they're threatened by them or they're afraid they'll want to control everything. I was petrified when I first got divorced, everyone kept telling me what a 'strong woman' I was and how difficult it was going to be because 'men don't like strong women, they want to be in control of everything'. I remember thinking, 'my God, I'll never find anyone who wants to be with me!' I may be really strong but I'm also really sensitive.

I've been pleasantly surprised to find there are a lot of men who appreciate the qualities in a successful and determined woman. I think some men quite like gutsy women who have something to fight for. Those men tend to be quite secure in themselves, I guess. They have confidence in their own ability; so as long as you're not competing with them, they don't perceive your strength as a threat. They also don't seem to mistake strength for coldness. No matter how strong you are, I think women will always be the nurturers. We'll never lose that. It's in our chemistry. It's part of our make-up.

donna hay

donna hay

Even the poshest French chef would concede that Australia is now one of the great modern food countries of the world. But Australia's fine food culture isn't limited to the first-rate fare dished out by our best restaurants. No, the real revolution is taking place in our kitchens at home.

Forget chops and boiled carrots — today you're more likely to find mussel and tomato risotto or rocket and ricotta pasta on the dining tables of many Australians. And that in part is thanks to Donna Hay, whose big-on-taste, low-on-preparation-time recipes are shaping the palettes of a new generation.

Credited with playing a pivotal role in the revival in home cooking, this 32-year-old culinary maven is currently the biggest selling cookbook author in Australia. In her mid-twenties Hay created the hugely successful *marie claire* cookbook series, the first of which went on to sell a million copies worldwide. She then launched her own magazine, *Donna Hay* and her next book, *off the shelf*, which shot to the bestseller list as soon as it came out in late 2001, and is still there. Hay's column in the *Sunday Telegraph*, which is syndicated across Australia, is read by millions of food lovers around the country every week.

When I was a kid my two older sisters and I would always pretend to make cakes in the kitchen and we'd make mud pies in our cubby house. Either for that reason, or maybe just because she wanted to get us out of her hair, when I was seven, Mum started sending us to a cooking school run by the local council during the school holidays. She used to go along to the adult classes. It was when microwaves first came out and I think she was quite excited about what she could do with one in the kitchen.

When I was a little older, Mum always encouraged me to cook. She didn't like cooking so I think she was overjoyed when one of her daughters showed some interest in it. She would bargain with me: 'If you cook dinner,' she'd say, 'I'll do all the cleaning up.' That sounded like a good deal to me — who wouldn't do anything to get out of the washing up! I used to make dinner for the whole family — things like spaghetti bolognaise and tuna mornay that I learnt from my little *Let's Learn to Cook* book. One of my greatest triumphs was the perfect steak diane I made for Dad's birthday. It was the late 1970s — steak diane was extremely trendy in those days and quite an achievement for an eight year old.

I came to cook for a living by default, really. I didn't like school very much so when I finished my HSC, I wasn't keen to go on to university. I did think about studying physiotherapy, but when the HSC marks came out I was two points short of the cutoff mark. Secretly, of course, I was quite relieved, but it did leave me at a loss about what I was going to do.

I decided I should do something I was already good at. Cooking was really easy for me but I knew I didn't want to be a home economics teacher — I couldn't bear putting up with badly behaved kids like me all day. And I didn't want to go into food science. The thought of wearing a lab coat every day and mixing chemicals in test tubes to come up with new flavours for snack foods made me shudder. I'd rather be making tuna mornay in a hospital cafeteria.

In the end, I did a home economics course at East Sydney TAFE. I expected it to be really dull but it wasn't.

There were lots of girls my age, really naughty girls from the country who'd gone to boarding schools. I was so innocent compared to them and they taught me a trick or two.

During class they'd steal other people's ingredients or turn down the ovens of the girls they didn't like, so their pies and cakes came out sloppy and wet. So by the end of class there'd be a few girls scratching their heads and wondering what went wrong while we'd giggle behind our tea towels in the corner.

Those country girls taught me so well that it wasn't long before I came to the attention of the head of the school. In those days, you had to wear a uniform to TAFE. Home economics students had to wear white dresses with stockings and petticoats, and awful sensible lace-up shoes. We looked just like nurses — I could have walked straight into a hospital and administered a drip to a patient and no one would have blinked an eye. We hated those uniforms. We were only 18 or 19 and wanted to wear something cool, not a replica of the outfit Matron Sloane wore on *A Country Practice.* In particular I couldn't get my head around the concept of the petticoat. Firstly, it was the late 1980s, not the 1800s, and the terrible lacy synthetic petticoat would rub against your pantihose and create static. I never wore mine. I refused to.

The teachers took the uniform rule very seriously. They took marks off your overall assessment if you wore the wrong shoes, or had a ladder in your stockings. I was always in trouble for my anti-petticoat protest. One teacher was particularly annoyed, so I thought, well, if she really wants me to wear a petticoat, I will. I bought the longest petticoat I could find — the lace trim hung 20 centimetres below the hem of my uniform, it was fantastic. I couldn't get much more petticoated than that!

This particular teacher also happened to be the head of the home economics school. She was a matronly woman and took her job quite seriously, like she was training Russian gymnasts for the Olympics, and my billowing petticoat was the last straw. She called me into her office one afternoon. 'Donna Hay!' she growled. 'You,' she paused for effect, 'will amount to nothing!'

About 10 years later I was invited to give a demonstration at the cooking school at the Sydney Fish Markets. I'd given demonstrations many times and found them quite easy and fun to do. Not long after I started this particular one, I noticed a familiar face in the audience. I couldn't quite place her at first and then it hit me — it was that teacher. She was sitting in the front row beaming like a proud mum. It really shook me for the first half hour — I got quite frightened and nervous and I was terrified of making a mistake in front of her! I remember I touched my hair and thought, oh no, I hope she didn't see that. At TAFE we were never allowed to touch our hair while we were cooking.

When I finished TAFE I did work experience in the recipe testing kitchen of *Women's Weekly*, and they offered me a job for three months to fill in for someone who was away. There was an in-house studio where all of the food was photographed and it was there that I met some of the freelance stylists who prepared and arranged the dishes for shoots. After those three months, I'd lined up enough freelance work to keep me busy for months and I've worked for myself ever since.

Things were very different then. It was the early 1990s and everything was photographed under hot lights and the shots were crammed with props. The food was virtually the last thing to be considered. It was almost like a formula, you could do it with your eyes shut. Any type of country dish had to be photographed with a bunch of wheat, and teacakes had to have a teapot and a vase of carnations in the background.

When I started styling, I followed the formula like everyone else. But after a while, I couldn't bear the sight of another crock-pot or floral napkin, so I started doing things the way I wanted to. I shot everything on white plates against white backgrounds. To begin with, most people thought it was too sterile, especially the clients who preferred the traditional style. They just couldn't see that the pictures were meant to be about the food, that what you're supposed to be looking at is how the chilli is meant to be chopped, or the difference between Thai basil and Italian basil so you know which one to buy at the fruit shop. Gradually they did come around to my way of thinking, once they realised that it was much easier to actually cook from the recipes when you could see the food properly in the pictures. And the food looked so much better without all of the frou frou props and tricks like spraying it with hairspray to keep it frozen in place.

It wasn't that long ago, but people thought so differently about food back then. I was a member of an organisation for people in the food media industry. It was a really diverse group, there were people from 21 to 100 years of age. One woman who had just come back from a trip to the UK proclaimed at one of the meetings that prepackaged meals were the future of food. All over London people were buying ready-prepared food, mashed potato and everything, she said, so Australia had better be prepared because it would happen here sooner or later and all of us would be lucky to have jobs when it did. Food, she said, will become like embroidery — a hobby for those who have the time and the inclination.

That was ridiculous. It was true that cooking wasn't really thought of as cool, but as for home-cooked meals being dead! In the late 1980s, eating out was indeed the thing to do — whether it was at a nice restaurant or one of the explosion of Indian or noodle takeaways that had popped up everywhere. But I think the reason for this was because people didn't know how to cook, which meant they didn't like doing it. Most of my friends didn't know how to cook because they were never taught; it was as if cooking was something that should just come naturally to a girl. Their mums would put the crock-pot on in the morning before they went to work and dinner was stewing by the time the kids got home from school in the afternoon.

Things started to change in the 1990s. Homewares became huge, people wanted to learn how to cook, they wanted to socialise with friends at home instead of sitting in restaurants with waiters hovering around. I could see all of that happening and it fuelled me to develop my own philosophy about food and how it should be presented. I started working with some young photographers who were okay about me wanting to try something new and different.

Becoming the food editor at *marie claire* magazine was a turning point. Funnily enough, it happened by complete chance. I was 25 and had been freelancing for about six years. Jane Roarty — a well-known Australian fashion stylist — was in town from London (where she was living then) to see the editor of *marie claire* about the fashion director's job, which she eventually took. She just happened to wander into the studio I shared with a couple of photographers and noticed my work. Jane really liked it and went back to *marie claire* and told the editor, Jackie Frank, that she had found her a food editor.

I went for an interview and that was it, the job was mine. I produced the food pages for the magazine from my own studio, and as long as I had my work in before deadline I was free to do whatever I wanted. *marie claire* had never had a food section so I could develop my own style. Walking into *marie claire* was frightening, though. I used to dread going to the office because I was the plain cooking girl amongst all the glamorous women dressed in Prada, Gucci and Louis Vuitton.

Murdoch Magazines, which owns *marie claire*, also has a book publishing division. I thought that what I was doing for the magazine — simple food real people could cook at home — would lend itself nicely to a cookbook. So I stepped across the corridor into executive chairman Matt Hanbury's office and told him I had an idea for a book.

The Murdoch Books people liked the idea but weren't sure if the book would sell and only wanted to print 12,000 copies. I think they were a little worried that I was so young; I mean, I doubt that they'd ever published a book by a girl in her mid-twenties. In those days most of the management was much older than me. My age has often been a problem for me, especially in the beginning. It was harder to get people to take me seriously, but that actually motivated me. It made me determined to prove them wrong. Anyway, the publisher assigned to me eventually convinced her superiors to print 20,000 copies of the book. *marie claire cooking*, which became the first of a series I did with Murdoch Books, went on to sell over a million copies around the world.

Now that I've got the magazine and a newspaper column and I'm doing more books, things are a lot more hectic. Initially I struggled with the business side of things, probably because I was more frightened of that aspect than anything else, but I got over that quite quickly. I work really closely with my creative director, Vanessa Holden, who has been with me the whole time. We're not scared of failure or of trying something new. Taking the safe road is so dull anyway. I don't want to be like one of those people who stand at the bus stop every morning with dreary looks on their faces, dreading going to work because it's so boring and repetitive. We try to break the rules and set our own course, otherwise we'll be just like everyone else in the business. You can sit back and hope for things to do well but they won't succeed if you don't continue pushing forward.

Joining a newspaper company was a real change for me. I was so used to working with magazine people, most of them women, and I didn't expect the newspaper world would be any different. The culture is very different, with different types of people in charge, and at first I had to make a real effort to be considered more than just someone who was good at cooking. It's very business oriented and I've made that step. I go to meetings prepared with notes, questions and solutions and I expect answers. I'm not timid — it's a waste of my time if I don't get to say what I think. It wasn't until I got some runs on the board that they sat up and really took notice. I remember we ran a little booklet of tips from *off the shelf* on the cover of the *Sunday Telegraph* and it lifted the newspaper's circulation by 30,000 copies. Things like that help to change people's perception of you.

But I haven't done it all on my own. Vanessa has been with me every step of the way since I left *marie claire* and started doing things under my own name. She is just so clever. When you imagine what a 'creative director' is like you think fluffy design-school dreamer, but Vanessa is not like that at all. She could have been a neurosurgeon if she'd wanted to. She is also my best friend. We met at *marie claire* where she was the director of the creative services department. I remember her being really different, quite odd even, but her intelligence shone through. Our strengths really complement each other.

I suppose it's unusual for best friends to work together, and it can be a bad idea for some people. But Vanessa and I don't hold back. We've had a couple of fisticuffs over the years but we're both such straight talkers that we don't let things fester and blow out of proportion. The worst thing you can do is not address a problem when it arises. You've got to let someone know when they've overstepped a boundary, or else you've only got yourself to blame for feeling miserable.

When we started the magazine we were both a little naive about the responsibilities of taking on staff. It had always been just the two of us who had generated everything and we didn't quite know what to do when more people were thrown into the equation. We had new roles and were both setting new boundaries. There was a lot of pressure on us in the early stages and it was probably the roughest time we've had as working partners. One day we left the office and we went to a café and got a lot of things off our chests quite publicly and even shed a few tears over it. We still give each other a hard time at work, but mostly it's just in fun. Having mutual respect for each other is important in a professional and personal friendship like ours.

The part of my job I find the strangest is being the face of everything. It's extremely weird seeing your picture in the newspaper and your name on the covers of piles of books when you're walking through a department store on the way to the lingerie department to stock up on undies.

The American book tour I went on last year (for *off the shelf*) was about as bizarre as it gets. It was my fourth author tour, but my first big one in America. I realised then you couldn't be shy and reserved. It doesn't make you look very good to the public and doesn't impress your publishers.

On that trip everything was riding on my big interview on the CBS 'Good Morning America' show.

Normally, knowing that millions of people were watching would make me nervous to the point of being sick but, strangely, I was quite calm. (Compared to facing the wrath of my publisher if the interview went badly, the interview seemed like a piece of cake.) CBS wanted me to cook a recipe from the book while we did the interview. Cooking and talking at the same time — getting across how *fantastic* it is, even remembering the title of the book, while looking at the cameras, chopping garlic and trying not to slice off the top of your finger — is very difficult. Luckily, this time, the pasta got cooked, the interview got done and my fingers survived unscathed.

When doing publicity events you almost have to create a separate persona. It's like being in a bad school play sometimes. You blow-dry your hair straight every morning and put on the layers of make-up and whenever you're asked, *everything* is of course *always* fantastic and you hear yourself using words like *brilliant* and *fabulous* all of the time. It's kind of like living in the third person. Still I'd rather come across like that than seem dull, especially on TV. Now I know why all of those people who do the advertorials on morning TV seem so overexcited about carpet cleaner.

The book tours are quite fun, but in the end, they're just work for me. They take me away from my work at the studio and my partner, Bill, at home. Bill is quite good about it all, though. We've been together for seven years, so he knew me long before anyone else knew who Donna Hay was. We got engaged a while back but we just can't seem to find the time for a wedding. Bill is from the country, he owns a cattle farm in Orange and a few butcher and produce shops in Sydney. Actually, that's how I met him. I used to buy the meat I used in photo shoots from one of his shops.

I remember thinking, this guy is getting a bit friendly with me. It didn't matter if I dropped into the shop at 6.30 in the morning, he was always so chirpy and happy to see me. I used to think the only thing worse than going out with your butcher would be dating your fishmonger, but clearly I got over that.

I wasn't surprised when he finally asked me out on a date. But he had to ask a few times before I said yes. I thought, oh well, why not. He took me on a pub crawl and it was the biggest disaster. We started in Paddington and before we got to the restaurant he had booked at Taylor Square in Darlinghurst I was already pretty light-headed — I'm not a big drinker and I get tipsy quickly.

On the way, he asked me what I didn't like to eat so that he'd know what to order when we sat down for dinner. 'I hate fried rice and I'm not really big on seafood,' I said. So what did Bill do? He ordered fried rice and barbecued mixed seafood. I found out later it was because he was so nervous. He was trying so hard to memorise 'seafood' and 'fried rice' that by the time the waiter came to take our order that was all he could remember. I didn't eat a thing and then we dropped into another bar on the way back to Paddington. I wasn't very well the next day, to say the least. It wasn't the best start but after that he sort of just grew on me. Of course, he tells a different story!

Bill is really supportive of my career but he doesn't like it when I go away on long trips. It's nice to come home to him at the end of it all — it's a reality check after all of the hoopla of publicity.

When I'm doing a stretch of long hours he'll go home in the middle of the day and do the washing or clean up, or he'll start cooking dinner if he gets home first. He's really lovely like that. He's very blokey and always happy and sees the bright side of things. Bill is the kind of guy who sees his cup as half-full, rather than half-empty. I'm the same, but I'm more inclined to think, 'Well, where the hell did the other half go and why can't I have it?' We have a good relationship. Bill definitely makes me a better person.

Bill's also really busy with his own business, which actually works quite well for our relationship because there is no finger pointing when one of us works back till 10.00 p.m. There are times when we hardly see each other. Most mornings I get up at four and work a 14-hour day at the studio, and sometimes I'll be working seven days straight for months on end. But that means we don't take the time we do have together for granted. It's more precious. The other good thing about it is that we rarely have time to fight.

Bill really wants children. Last year for Christmas he gave me a baby car seat, just as a gentle little reminder. I thought it was hilarious, that's just his sense of humour. At least we've got one less item to shop for when we finally do decide to take the plunge.

I do want kids too, I love them. I'm just not sure how I'll be able to fit motherhood into everything else I'm committed to. I'm hoping I'll find a way. Being a perfectionist doesn't help. I want to know that when I have a child I'll still be able to do all the things I'm doing now and do them perfectly. It's a bit frightening because I'm already so stretched across everything. I don't spend a lot of time with my family as it is. I've got two young nieces who I'd like to see more of and I've lost contact with some of my old friends.

I wonder how I would do it all, but then, as Vanessa points out, I'm already up at 4.00 a.m. every morning anyway. Actually, it's a really lovely hour of the morning. I do a few hours' work at home and then go for a walk at 6.00 a.m. and I'm at the studio by 8.00 a.m. I get to have that part of my day all to myself before I come to work.

Sometimes, when I'm having one of my dark moments about the drawbacks of being female, I think about how women are expected to do so much — to be the nurturer, the carer and the businesswoman as well.

I've been thinking about that a lot lately since all of the debate over whether women should be entitled to paid maternity leave. I've always worked for myself or on contract and I've never been pregnant so I had no idea that some women don't get paid maternity leave. It just seems wrong. Vanessa has two children, her youngest was born this year, and she brought him to work with her when he was five weeks old. I would rather have her here with the baby than not have her here at all.

You do have to sacrifice certain things in order to have a career like this — with or without children. I know it's hard for the people in your life when you can't always be available for them. Some of my friends are really understanding and make light of it, but others take it personally, as if I've changed somehow now that I've become well known.

I do love what I do, but saying that, I know I'd be fine if it all disappeared tomorrow. I would be quite happy as a mum doing canteen duty twice a week and playing tennis every Wednesday. It wouldn't bother me at all because I'm not so addicted to this lifestyle that I wouldn't cope without it. I'm not scared of change either. I quite like it, so I know I could quite happily do something else. I like getting on with things — I don't spend too much time contemplating, I think it's unhealthy.

There are some moments in my life when I stop and think, 'God, it really has been amazing.' I might be walking through Harrods in London and see a stack of my books and have a giggle to myself. It's good fun. I'm so lucky. I get to work with my friends and we all get along so well. Everyone I work with loves to eat — and we do a lot of that in the studio, testing recipe after recipe. People are always stopping by for cups of tea and there's never any shortage of biscuits and cakes to munch on. We have a big table in the studio and we sit around and have lunch together like a big family. And when one of us needs time-out, there's a big comfy lounge to lie on. All of the people I work with make my business what it is, so I'm really conscious that they're happy and that I look after them.

The most important thing, I think, is to make sure you don't take things too seriously. You've got to laugh at yourself and take everything for what it is. We come up with recipes, cook those recipes and photograph some of them — that's it, we're not formulating a plan for world peace!

elizabeth macgregor

elizabeth macgregor

Scotland-born Macgregor has called Australia home since 1999, when, amid a flurry of press interest, she arrived in Sydney to take up the post of director at the Museum of Contemporary Art.

Macgregor inherited an institution that was not only embroiled in politics, but looking directly down the barrel of bankruptcy. Needless to say, the expectations of her were immense and both the arts community and the media kept an eye permanently fixed on what had become a saga-like situation. Could this enthusiastic Scot, everyone wondered, save one of Australia's most ailing artistic institutions?

It wasn't the first time Macgregor had been handed the task of resurrecting an institution in a bind. In England, she is credited with elevating Birmingham's Ikon Gallery to national prominence, and has developed an impressive reputation for bringing contemporary art to a wider audience.

My first memory of art was being dragged around the Kelvingrove Art Gallery in Glasgow. My parents are originally from Glasgow so they would take us there every year during the school holidays and we'd go to the gallery on rainy days. I remember seeing this incredible Salvador Dali painting. That memory is still so vivid in my mind.

I grew up in the Orkney Islands, which are right up off the north coast of Scotland. They're quite remote, to get there you drive as far as you can and then take a boat. There's an incredible sense of history on the islands, including prehistoric remains and evidence of the islands' tumultuous history with the Vikings and various Norse earls. It's very beautiful and a wonderful place to grow up. I went to a fantastic school — the islands attract a very high calibre of teachers, some of them Orkney natives who have come back to the islands after living elsewhere, and others from the mainland who have moved there to drop out of the rat race.

Aside from those trips to the art museums in Glasgow, I had very few encounters with art when I was growing up. I was much more interested in music. Until I was 15 I planned to go to music school, but I changed my mind when my mathematics teacher told me it would be a shocking waste of a good brain. I decided to study languages instead, but I always kept up my love of music.

I enrolled in French and Italian at Edinburgh University but I needed to find another subject, which is how I eventually fell into art. Being a typical student, I perused the curriculum for what I thought would be the easiest option, with no early morning or lunchtime lectures of course. I wound up choosing Art History. I knew nothing about it but it fitted quite nicely into my no-early-morning-starts criteria, so that was it.

Little did I suspect that I would become so entranced that I would change my course after a year to major in it. I kept up my French and Italian and spent my summers working and travelling in Italy. I love Italy, especially Rome with its wonderful Renaissance and Baroque art and architecture.

Funnily enough, once I finished my degree I still knew nothing about contemporary art — I think my course stopped around the 1920s. I did some voluntary work at the National Gallery of Scotland while I was studying and I think that set me on my path. I worked on education programs with children and I became very interested in how you could encourage people to become involved with art.

My parents expected me to have a career. I was always encouraged to go to university. I have a brother and two sisters and my parents believed very strongly in the importance of an education. They would have discouraged me from getting married too young like a lot of girls still did in the late 1970s and early 1980s. But then my parents are not your typical, middle-class conservative Scots — I didn't marry until I was almost 30 and I don't have children, and none of that has ever been an issue for them. I'm fortunate that one of my sisters has three children so they haven't missed out on the experience of being grandparents.

My parents were always forward-thinking, which is interesting and surprising to some people when they find out that my father worked for the church. He was a minister in the Church of Scotland as I grew up. People expect me to have had an austere or repressive childhood but it really wasn't like that at all. My father went into the church quite late in life and he was a very politically engaged man. He didn't get bogged down in all of the rules and regulations of the church, he was much more interested in the humanitarian elements of religion.

Dad was pretty easy-going on us. We did have to go to church every Sunday — as a minister's daughter you couldn't get out of things like that. But I learnt to play the organ so I could sit with my back to the congregation and read a book during the boring parts!

Looking back on it, I think my parents were remarkably open-minded and sanguine about having to cope with the rebellious teenager that I was. They are very tolerant people — tolerant of other people's attitudes and as church people they are very open to other religions. They've never rammed their religion down other people's throats. More than anything, my parents brought us up to be considerate of other people. Our family was always doing things like fostering children, not just Scottish kids but kids from all different racial backgrounds.

I suppose my father was quite a rebel. He was constantly challenging the church. He would do things like organise activities on a Sunday, which didn't go down very well with the fundamentalists in the community who steadfastly believed that Sunday was a day of rest, as the Bible declares. He is very liberal in his outlook and always openly supportive of women priests and gays in the church.

At one stage, he became so disillusioned with the outdated rules and regulations of the Church of Scotland that he left. He became a teacher and taught religious studies for a while. Eventually, he went back to the church but not to the Church of Scotland. He joined the Scottish Episcopal Church, which is similar to the Anglican Church. It's less austere than the Presbyterian Church of Scotland. I was in my thirties when he was made a bishop, to our astonishment! The family was quite shocked at first as he hardly seemed the type to go for all that pomp and circumstance. They'd been living in a very poor area in Edinburgh at the time. But it seemed that there was a specific task for him to do as a bishop so he went.

I'm very close to my father and I find it hard to be so far away from Scotland, especially now that he is very ill. But he is the kind of man who would hate for me not to get on with my own life or give up an opportunity for his sake. He'd much rather that I live in Australia doing something I love than have me living across the road and doing a job I didn't find fulfilling. He always used to warn me about working too hard and ironically he had a stroke when he retired at 65.

My parents have always been supportive of my career. They didn't bat an eyelid when I informed them that my first job out of university involved driving around Scotland in a bright green and red double-decker bus. The bus was actually a travelling art gallery run by the Scottish Arts Council. A friend saw the ad for a curator/driver in the paper and sent it to me. I was only 22 and I knew nothing about contemporary art or Scottish art but I went for the job anyway. My friend coached me a little bit the night before the interview. I guess they were impressed with my enthusiasm and thought they'd give this woman who never stopped talking a shot. I'm probably the only person in the art world who spent the first three weeks of their career learning to drive a lorry and sitting for a heavy vehicle licence so I could drive a bus.

The Travelling Gallery was designed to take art to places where there were no galleries or where people might not consider going to galleries, like housing estates and prisons. I guess that's where my religious background comes in — I was on a mission to take art to the people. I used to joke with my father that it showed how alike we were — he was trying to convert people to religion and I was trying to convert them to art.

I drove the bus all over Scotland for three years. It was actually rather beautiful inside. It was a normal double-decker but it had been cut off at the chassis and a new structure put on top to create one big, single-storey open space. We'd hang pictures on the walls but often stacked two or three high. Otherwise it was just like a normal gallery. I would organise the exhibitions, plan the tour and then take it all on the road. I'm still the only person I know who can do a three-point turn in a double-decker bus in the snow!

It was great fun for a 22 year old. I'd drive into town, plug in the electricity and everybody passing would wander in for a look. The response was amazing. People didn't know it was a gallery so we had a lot of visitors who would never normally think of setting foot into one. They came without any expectations. It was a great training ground because most curators don't have that kind of constant contact with the public. I really enjoyed seeing how people responded to the work.

It was fascinating. My first observation was that people don't automatically object to contemporary art or modern art. They were prepared to take a look and were, above all, curious about what they saw. They'd chat about the works and argue about them which I think is very healthy — people are so much more open-minded than the media ever gives them credit for. The media goes on and on about how 'ordinary' people can't relate to contemporary art, but it's just not true. It depends on the context you show it in and what kind of information you provide. You have to make people feel welcome. I think a lot of galleries, particularly the contemporary galleries, can be very intimidating. They can make people feel like idiots for not understanding the works, or worse, that they're being conned. Sometimes I would take the artists along and they would give talks about the work and meet visitors. It was all about overcoming myths about art.

I found that in remote areas, the hunger for knowledge and information was huge. I think those communities really appreciated the fact that somebody was going to the trouble to take something to them, even if it wasn't something they immediately liked. I would discover potential art lovers in the most unlikely places, like prisons. At the time, Scotland had an incredible art program running in Barlinnie Prison, one of the hardest gaols in the country. One of the inmates there, a famous gangland murderer called Jimmy Boyle, actually became a sculptor while he was in gaol and eventually, when he was released, went on to have great success as an artist. I think a lot of those programs have gone now, but they were incredible at the time. They worked on the belief that art could help rehabilitate people and teach them new ways of looking at and dealing with the world. It was controversial but I happen to believe in it too. I think art has enormous healing powers. Unleashing a person's creativity through art is a way of channelling what might otherwise be very negative energy.

The prisons were probably more open to art than a lot of places. Some of schools we visited were much harder to crack, especially the tough inner-city schools full of bored teenagers who just didn't want to be there.

I remember on one occasion going to two different schools in a new town called Livingstone, which was quite a tough place. The first school was totally horrendous. I couldn't get the kids to engage on any level. The next day I went to the other school, with a very similar demographic but the kids could not have been more different. These 14-year-old boys were unbelievable; they still gave me a hard time, but they were articulate, they questioned things and they wanted to know more about what they were seeing. They were critiquing the work. They wanted to know what on earth the artist thought he was doing calling some pigment and a few sticks 'art'.

It was amazing how two very similar schools could be so different, but it came down to just one man, an art teacher. This guy was an inspiration. He gave those kids a vocabulary to talk about art and the confidence to talk about ideas. It made me realise just how powerful working with art could be. If you work with kids that are young enough, art can help them develop communication skills and self-confidence, abilities we all need to get by in the world.

The Travelling Gallery was so successful that the Arts Council decided to invest in a brand-new, purpose-built bus when the old one began falling to bits. I did some research and discovered a number of other examples of mobile museums in Europe. There was a library equivalent, an education van in Bordeaux and a few others, but none concentrated on art. To my knowledge, our bus was the only one like it in the world at that stage. However, I recently met a man from regional New South Wales who has converted a horse trailer to a mobile gallery so maybe there will be a Museum of Contemporary Art bus one of these days!

Towards the end of my days on the bus, I was exhausted. It was an incredible experience but I was away from home a lot which made it difficult to maintain a life.

Actually I was so involved that the bus was my entire life. It happened to all of us who went into the arts — you went into a job and it became everything.

And my life continued like that. It wasn't until I came to Australia that I'd even considered the concept of work–life balance. Drawing the line between work and play is very hard in the visual arts: even when you're not working, you need to be visiting exhibitions, reading art magazines, going to exhibition openings, meeting artists and patrons. It's quite hard to get away from, even though these are things other people might not regard as work because they're fun to do. And it's a great privilege to meet artists from all over the world. Even now, I can never work out where work stops and fun starts.

Until recently, all the people I'd had long relationships with had been involved in the arts. My ex-husband, who I was married to for 12 years, was a museum director. We met in London, where I moved when I left the Scottish Arts Council to take up a job with the Arts Council of Great Britain. Not long after we married we moved from London to Birmingham. I was offered the director's job at the Ikon Gallery, and my husband found a job as director of the gallery in a nearby town. Initially, I balked at the idea of moving to Birmingham. I always said I wouldn't live there in a million years because it was such a horrible city — superficially anyway. But the Ikon had such an interesting history; it had supported many British artists and had a strong educational emphasis but it lacked any profile within the city.

Eventually I became very fond of Birmingham. It was a city that had been destroyed, bombed in the war, and then finished off by the city planners with hideous 1960s architecture. When I arrived, the City Council really wanted to change things. It was also incredibly interesting from a cultural point of view; it was hugely diverse. One in four of the population was not white — there was a very large Asian and African population. As with many cities at the end of the 1980s, there had been rioting and unrest in areas of social deprivation. Art was probably the last thing on anybody's mind and I was very interested in how you could make a contemporary art gallery relevant to a city full of people who were apparently indifferent to it. The challenge was to introduce contemporary art to a wider audience. My experience on the bus had led me to believe that you don't have to stoop to populism in the lowest common denominator to interest people. Contemporary art can be complex and challenging work, you just have to find ways for people to access it. You've got to try to get people to engage with art on all levels, to approach it with an open mind and to trust their own responses.

I was 30 when I first arrived at the Ikon and I stayed there for 10 years. I suppose I was quite young to be a director of a major public gallery, but not many people wanted to go to Birmingham. If it had been London, there would have been a lot more competition for a job like that.

At the time, most museum and gallery directors were men. Then in the early 1990s the situation changed as a lot of women became directors, except when it came to the national museums and galleries. They were, and have continued to be, run by men, apart from the Victoria and Albert Museum, which was run by a woman for a brief period in the mid-1990s.

To be honest, though, I'm not interested in running one of those institutions. It's a question of scale — the larger the institution, the further away you are from the art. The top job in a major international institution is more about staff management, bureaucracy and fundraising than it is about art and audiences. Of course it would be a much more powerful position to run a major international gallery, but I'm not interested in power just for the sake of it. I don't think many women are, maybe that's why there are still so few women in those positions. I know a lot of women in the art world who think the same. They're happy to forgo the power and prestige of a job at somewhere like the Tate for a post at a smaller gallery where they can focus on working with artists and not be so distant from their staff, or have to spend all their energies on fundraising.

Fundraising is tough for everyone. I remember having a conversation with a male colleague who ran a similar institution and he said, 'Oh, it's easy for you women, you just flirt with the guys and get the money.' But that's precisely the problem. Yes, it is sometimes easier for a woman to get access to businessmen (and they are still usually men!) and to hold their attention, but when it comes to closing the deal it is much harder. A lot of men still don't take women seriously when it comes to money and business. It's not universal, it doesn't happen everywhere, and to be fair there are some very enlightened people in business, but there is still an incredible chauvinism within the business world, especially in Australia.

In 20 years in England I never found myself in a position where I felt I wasn't being taken seriously because I was a woman. Yet when I came here, I found myself in meetings where I knew none of the men around the table were actually listening to me, even when I was the only one in the room who knew what I was talking about — my 20 years of experience didn't seem to count for much.

I encountered a number of men, many of whom were trying to be helpful, who clearly didn't think that I had any idea how to solve the problems of the MCA and in a variety of ways, some subtle and others not so subtle, they let me know it. My first few months here were a really testing time for me — some people just would not accept my authority as the director. At one point, I thought there must have been something wrong with me. I remember being relieved when I expressed my feelings to a businesswoman, an American who also works in Sydney. 'Is it really hard here or is it just me?' I asked. A look of recognition swept across her face. 'It is *so* hard here,' she said. 'I don't think they even do it consciously. It's got to be a cultural thing.'

I think that's true a lot of the time. Sometimes the chauvinism is so subtle that it's difficult to recognise. I remember one particular meeting I had with a well-meaning adviser when I first arrived. It was a difficult situation because I knew that everything he was suggesting wouldn't work. He was a very successful and powerful businessman, so I was very tactful in pointing out that his suggestions probably wouldn't work for us. The meeting went on for an hour and a half and I thought it had been a complete disaster as I didn't accept one of his ideas, but he seemed quite pleased with himself. A female colleague was also in the meeting and when he left she said, 'Did you not notice what happened? He came right round to your opinion. He started off saying one thing and he finished off saying another, which is exactly what you told him, so he's passed off your ideas as his own. Now he's gone home thinking that he's been a wonderful help to you and that *his* ideas saved the day.' She was right, but I hadn't even noticed and I don't think he did either. That kind of exchange would never happen between two men. A man would never allow another man to take credit for his ideas, especially in his presence. I don't think we'll ever get to the stage where men and women communicate in the same way as men communicate with each other, certainly in business. It's just a different dynamic between men and women and there are pluses and minuses to that.

In my case, I don't think it was just about sexism. It was a combination of things — the fact that they were dealing with the arts, which are generally regarded as not really competent in a business sense, and the troubled history of the MCA and the perception that it wasn't doing well financially didn't help.

When the head-hunter first approached me about the MCA, I said I wasn't interested because I'd just reopened the Ikon in its splendid new premises and I wanted to run it for a while. But after some deliberation, I decided to come to Sydney for the interview with the MCA board. It was a gamble to take the job and I knew it, but I decided to take the risk and give it a go. If it all failed dismally and I had to go crawling back to the UK then I'd just live with it. I believed it was worth the risk.

I had a very high regard for the MCA and I'd already been to Australia a number of times. I was intrigued that an institution with such a great international reputation, in such a wonderful city, could be in such trouble. I was well aware that the Museum had gone through a very difficult period financially following the end of the financial involvement of the University of Sydney and that to secure its future would be a great challenge. What I probably underestimated was how difficult it would be to get all of the parties involved to sit down together and discuss the best solution for the Museum. In those first dire six months, as the MCA was looking down the barrel of bankruptcy, I quickly realised that there were often other political games being played out, with the Museum as the pawn in the middle. Decoding the politics was difficult enough but trying to work around them just about drove me nuts.

Thanks to some loyal supporters and sponsors, we survived. We were bailed out of that initial crisis but it took another two years before the State Government finally agreed to support us, which is what we were seeking in the first place. It was only when the announcement was made that I realised how far we'd come: there wasn't a hint of criticism from any quarter. It was a very different story from when I first arrived and news broke that Carr was stepping in to keep the MCA afloat for another six months. All hell broke loose. The talkback hosts went nuts, so did the *Telegraph*, even the *Herald*. The headlines were horrendous — 'The Gallery that no one goes to ...', 'Nice building, shame about the art' and 'Money for wankers not miners' — because the Premier had just turned down a subsidy for a mine. It was the kind of furore you'd expect from the British tabloids.

I was astounded at the level of press interest in what was going on. A lot of it landed on my shoulders and that was very new to me. I had never had to conduct myself in the public eye in that way before. Two months after I arrived I was sitting in a bar and a complete stranger approached me and asked if I was the director of the MCA. It was 2.00 in the morning! I couldn't believe it. At one point I even started wearing a wig.

I'd find myself on the front page of the newspaper for some innocuous comment I'd made in what I believed to be an informal chat with a journalist. I quickly learnt that 'off the record' doesn't mean very much here and just how vicious some of the newspaper columnists could be. At one point there was a lot of misunderstanding over our relationship with the City Council and the Lord Mayor's plans for the Museum. Miranda Devine ripped into me. I was so surprised. I remember thinking, 'So much for female solidarity.' I guess that was a bit naive!

Now that the crisis is over the press has lost interest, but to be quite honest, I'm still very wary. I'm half expecting the tall poppy syndrome to come into play at any moment. Now that I've been successful in securing the Museum's future, maybe the knives will come out. I hope not, but you can never predict these things.

Just before I left England, I was talking to a friend who had spent some time working in Sydney. I asked him what he thought of it. 'Sydney,' he said, 'is a snake pit.' Sydney certainly has its reputation. People kept telling me that my job would be so much easier if the MCA was in Melbourne. 'Sydney is too busy. It's too beautiful. It doesn't need culture, it's got the harbour,' everyone would say. I remember George Miller telling me, not long after I arrived that Melbourne was where the ideas came from. 'You'll never get support for the MCA in Sydney,' he said. 'When you go to a dinner party in Melbourne everybody is sitting around the table talking ideas. When you go to a dinner party in Sydney, they're out on the balcony looking at the views of the harbour, talking about real estate prices.' After living here for three years, I can say that there is some truth in that.

Despite its reputation of superficiality, I have found Sydney to be a wonderful place. I have found many people to be not only supportive but incredibly hospitable and genuine. Australians are quick to develop friendships, they're not stand-offish like people are in London. You get to know people superficially in the art world there, but you never really get to know each other. There's also a great hunger for information. People really want to be informed about art. I'm delighted to have proved wrong all those people who told me that Sydney was not a city to support a contemporary art museum. In the past two years, we've seen attendances rise dramatically and they continue to rise. There is an audience for contemporary art here, just as there is all over the world. Australia is no different. It's also a young audience — young people have no problem identifying with contemporary art.

Coming to Australia was really the start of a new life for me. I was married when I came out and my husband had talked about coming here. But it didn't work out. I guess moving to Australia gave me the space to realise that our relationship wasn't working. I was lucky enough to meet someone else here and for the first time in my life I am with a man who is not in the art world. It's interesting because I've discovered that being close to someone who exists in a completely different industry can give you a tremendous sense of self-renewal. It makes you realise that there is indeed a life outside of your career. He was also a great comfort at the height of the MCA difficulties, when I really thought it was all going to go wrong. He managed to give me a sense of perspective on it all.

Perhaps the reason why I've never had children is because I was fortunate to find such a fulfilling profession. I'm 44 now and I don't regret not having children. I never made a conscious decision about it. In fact both my ex-husband and I expected we would have kids, but there was always something more urgent. It's not that I don't like children, I have nephews and nieces and I love them dearly. Sometimes I get a little nostalgic and think it might have been nice but mostly it's not something that bothers me now, in fact I'm quite glad that things have turned out this way. I wouldn't have had the life I have if I had children to care for, or at the very least, it would have made things much harder. It would have been much more difficult to do something like pack up and move to Australia. Maybe I'm lucky to have found a vocation that I am so passionate about.

I think it's still very difficult for a woman to reach the top of the ladder if she has a family. The fact is, to get there a woman needs to work as hard as a man and having a family to care for makes that almost impossible. If the culture continues that you can only get to the top by working ridiculous hours, then women are never going to get there. I've got a lot of close friends who have children and they just don't want to do both any more.

I think people overlook the fact that men face that pressure as well; climbing to the top means that they miss out on family life too. How many sad men do you know who barely see their wife and kids because they leave home at seven in the morning and don't get home until late at night? When you think about it like that, you realise that it's not actually a gender issue, it's an issue about corporate culture. If corporate culture (and indeed the arts culture) expects people to work these long hours, family life will suffer. As will relationships. There's no getting around that. I also believe that people do work better if they have other interests. And the idea of people working such long hours when there is so much unemployment is rather obscene. Surely we can find a way for people to earn a good living without the need for an all-encompassing work culture.

This requires a radical change in attitudes — it's not one that many big organisations would welcome, especially in their senior, highly paid staff. And I do think it is especially hard for women to effect change. I once worked for a wonderfully inspirational man at the Arts Council of Great Britain. He would refuse to go to breakfast meetings called by his superiors, because he took his children to school in the mornings. They would say, 'Doesn't your wife do that?' 'Actually, she's my partner, and no she doesn't, I take our children to school,' he would reply. No woman in his position could have put her family first like that and got away with it. She would have been accused of not coping or not being able to manage her professional and personal responsibilities. The whole culture needs to change and for that to happen we need more men to stand up against it. Men need time with their children (and partners) too.

I don't have any problem with women choosing to give up their careers, if that's what they want. My sister gave up work so she could dedicate herself to her children and I totally admire her for that. I couldn't have done it, but at the same time, I'd like to think that if I'd had children I wouldn't have worked the hours that I did.

It's a terrible conundrum really. In the end I suppose we all have to try and make what contribution we can. I would like to think that the MCA supports men and women to enjoy and feel fulfilled in their work but also have time for a life.

gale edwards

gale edwards

When Adelaide-born theatre director Gale Edwards, already a successful director in Australia, directed a production of Andrew Lloyd Webber's *Aspects of Love* in Sydney, she had no idea that it would lead her to Lloyd Webber himself and one of the most stellar international careers of any Australian theatre director.

Throughout the 1990s Edwards lived between London and New York where she directed musicals on the West End and Broadway, as well as works of opera, Shakespeare and drama for some of the great artistic companies of the world including The Royal Shakespeare Company and the English National Opera. As a woman, Edwards has achieved a string of firsts including being the first female director to work for Andrew Lloyd Webber. Along with playwright Nick Enright and Ben Gannon, she also created the hugely successful landmark Australian musical *The Boy from Oz*.

After a decade spent moving speedily about the world from gig to gig, Edwards recently moved back to Australia, where she is now based. She continues to direct theatre in Australia and around the world.

I grew up in Adelaide, in a working-class family that had no interest in, or access to, books, music, art or theatre. It was an unhappy home life, my father was an alcoholic, so I escaped into a rich fantasy world. When I was orphaned at age nine, I went to live with my maternal grandmother who brought me up. She was an usherette in the Hoyts cinemas and used to take me with her to work most nights and on weekends — imagine what that was like for a kid with my kind of imagination! I saw the same movies over and over and never got bored. I learnt to look for details around the edge of the frame. I swear it was the best training a director could get.

During the years I lived with my grandmother I excelled at school, where I was tagged to study Medicine or Law. But for as long as I can remember, all I ever wanted to do was work in the theatre. I wanted to be an actress, because nobody knew what a director was in those days. My grandmother wanted me to be an air hostess, a sensible job for a girl. When she died, I was 17 and, instead of following the academic life that my grades prepared me for, I went to Flinders University to study Drama as part of an Arts degree. I've been very independent ever since, but I think I have really missed not having a family, especially at times of needing support.

I was 21 in 1975 and there were so few opportunities to get into theatre, especially in Adelaide, so at the end of my three-year course the only path that seemed open to me was to become a drama teacher. Then, as fate would have it, I was posted to a new open-space high school that prized itself on its fabulous new drama studio and facilities and had an open-minded headmaster who encouraged the arts. I got to direct the big school musical every year and develop some specialist drama training for kids with an obvious bent for it. I virtually wrote the curriculum which became the basis for a Year 12 course in later years.

Finally, still feeling the passion to 'do' it myself, rather than teach, I ran away to London at age 26 to study and absorb English culture and arts and to do The Grand Tour of Europe. I revelled in seeing so *much* theatre. The lights of the West End were so seductive — here at last was a society where theatre was a major feature! And the British loved the classics, and did them very well, so this is where my own love affair with classical plays began. I sat in 'the Gods' at the very top of the auditorium, in the cheap one-pound seats, almost every night of the week — watching, learning, dreaming ...

When the money ran out (I was supporting myself on savings from the teaching years), I reluctantly returned to Australia knowing that things would never be the same. I could not just slip back into my former life. The 'theatre bug' had bitten and there was no antidote.

I realised on arriving back in Adelaide that I knew no one in the theatre and had no way in. I remember seeing Geoffrey Rush in the Adelaide Festival Theatre green room and being too coy to go up and speak to him. I could not have known then that only a few years later he would be playing The Fool in my *King Lear* with John Gaden on the main stage at the South Australian Theatre Company. But all that was in the future.

Determined not to be stopped, and fired by my experiences in Europe, I decided to try out some of the ideas I had from my time in London and, in order to do so, I formed my own theatre company, which I called Energy Connection. I used current and former high school students who had excelled at drama and we worked full-time for two years, mainly for no pay, creating major works which we staged at various festivals around Adelaide, which won us quite a local reputation. I was totally obsessed with the fascinating work of running a company and creating original theatre using dance and image and spoken word. I was also teaching the company on a day-to-day basis. Many of those Energy Connection members went on to have careers in the Australian theatre — Tony Poli, Mark Pegler, Leverne McDonald, Jonathan Mill, Dean Carey, to name a few.

We were young and we didn't care about things like money then. We believed what we were doing was important and it was challenging and fun. Outside of the theatre company, we were all unemployed and living off the dole. We did it because we loved the theatre. We didn't ask the hard questions like: How am I going to live? How am I going to pay the rent? We lived in each other's houses; we just got by whatever way we could. I remember sitting around on the floor of my flat, with some of the actors, sharing a flagon (remember *flagons*? It *was* the 1970s!) of red wine discussing concepts and writing scripts, with hundreds of pages strewn all over the place. All of us were contributing and creating. It was a phenomenal time, born out of innocence and passion and, dare I say it, naivety.

For a small company made up of virtual amateurs, we actually did extremely well. We were given our own theatre space to work in by the South Australian Government

Youth and Education Department, called Theatre 62, and we created six full-scale productions over two years in major theatres, and toured them around South Australia for the Arts Council. We even toured some of them to Sydney. Eventually, we got funding from the State Government and Federal Government but, after two intense years, it was time for all of us to move on.

If I saw those shows today, perhaps I'd cringe, but at the time they made a real impact and we were considered very avant-garde in Adelaide. I was inspired by Peter Brook's work. We all read his book *The Empty Space*, which was about his ideas on theatre, and were filled with a genuine youthful idealism that I have looked back on with nostalgia over the years. We were in touch with something very vital in those days. Sometimes I miss that quality today — the sheer bloody commitment and determination!

John Clark, who is head of the National Institute of Dramatic Art, heard about the company, and came to see the shows. He watched me run it for two years from nothing, without funding, and put it on the map. So one day John invited me to move to Sydney and do the director's course at NIDA. I remember saying, 'No. Why would I want to do that? I'm running this company here in Adelaide.' His response was brief and to the point. 'Because you don't know anything. What you have is great bravura and passion, and good ideas and maybe even some vision, but you don't actually *know* anything.' He was right. I'd gone just about as far as I could on my own, I needed to learn from someone who *did* know something.

I moved to Sydney in 1981 and did the year-long director's course. Once it was over, John asked me to stay on at NIDA as a teacher and Nick Enright asked me to direct the graduation play that year — a new musical he'd written with Terry Clarke called *Summer Rain*. I taught at NIDA for five years alongside highly skilled theatre practitioners like Nick Enright, one of Australia's most prolific playwrights and now a long-time friend and collaborator (we did *The Boy from Oz* together a decade and a half later). I also had the opportunity to work on classical texts with brilliant voice teachers at my side like Betty Williams, Bill Pepper and the late Doreen Cannon, who all taught me so much about text and language and structure.

In fact, I learnt more as a teacher at NIDA than I did as a student. I still joke with John that I'm the only person who has ever done a *six*-year NIDA course! I came out understanding a lot about the theatre, in terms of language especially — from Chekhov to Brecht, from David Mamet to Patrick White — but also practical knowledge from working with actors. It was such a privilege and advantage to be working in a 'laboratory' with acting students all day every day. I learnt so much about actors' needs, how vulnerable they are, how courageous they are, how extraordinary they are. I learnt about how important 'process' is.

It was invaluable to have those years at NIDA, especially to have the opportunity to work on and direct classical texts which, in those days, were rare enough in Australia and mainly the premise of men. I don't know what would have happened to me if I hadn't gone there. There were few opportunities for a woman of my age and experience then. A one-year postgraduate directing course at NIDA was helpful, but it didn't make me a director. Being a director is not something you can learn at school. You become a director by doing it and it helps if someone believes in you enough to nurture you. And at NIDA I was nurtured and given copious directing opportunities and chances to work beside well-known directors who came as guests.

Then I met John Gaden, who at the time was the artistic director of the South Australian Theatre Company. I was in Adelaide for The Festival of Arts directing a brand-new Australian musical, which was going badly, and we met over lunch and laughed a lot and just clicked. The very next day he invited me to come back to Adelaide as his associate director for the company. John is a great actor, a very generous collaborator, a great facilitator, and a statesman for the theatre. He encouraged me to be as involved in everything as I could be, and so I gained an insight into the running of a State company, as well as directing many wonderful plays over the two years that I was there.

Looking back I think it's interesting that the two people who gave me those first crucial breaks were men: John Clark and John Gaden. Three, if you count that amazing headmaster, Joe Laslett, who encouraged me to create Energy Connection. It's interesting because at the time — we're talking 20 years ago now — there were so few theatre company directors giving women directors any kind of encouragement or support, let alone a chance to actually direct a play for them. This was the early 1980s, before affirmative action, before it became imperative to employ women if you wanted to qualify for grants. I had no female mentors. There were virtually no women directing for the major State companies. There might be *one* in an entire year's repertoire but the play would usually be relegated to the small studio space, instead of playing on the main stage, or perhaps the woman was a famous actress who was allowed to direct, like Robyn Nevin.

The excuse the theatre company directors always gave was that there were no women directors to choose from. How could there be? Interestingly, Sue Hill and Christine Westwood, who ran the Nimrod Theatre back in the 1970s before it became the Belvoir St Theatre in 1984, said the same thing. That was the era that produced Neil Armfield, but looking back at the statistics, very few women were given the opportunity to work as directors at the Nimrod of the 1970s. Even fewer worked at the Sydney Theatre Company during Richard Wherrett's 11-year tenure through the 1970s into the 1980s.

That was the climate I came up through. The world has changed a lot since then, so it's a very different situation in the theatre now. Twenty years later there are plenty of women directing at the major State companies and a few of them are now run by women. These days, every theatre company has to have a good percentage of women directors in their repertoire to be kosher; to attract funding, to look like they're supporting affirmative action. And also because women have proved that they are very *good* directors!

It was not so when I was coming up through the ranks. In the early 1980s, every time I walked into a rehearsal room for the initial day I'd come face to face with a cast of actors who had never worked with a woman director before. It was the first time those actors had looked up and seen a woman out the front. And there were teething problems. Even years later at the Royal Shakespeare Company in London, I remember one British old boy feeling very insecure about being directed by a woman, let alone an *Australian* woman! And he made that quite clear in the rehearsals. Until I wore him down over the following weeks and he finally ended up raving about working with me. But it was a battle.

John Gaden was one of the first directors of a major theatre company to give a woman a break, and it was mid-1980 before that happened. John was interested in nurturing talent. He wasn't one of those men who is resentful of or threatened by another person's talent. He encouraged me to do whatever I wanted and gave me the opportunity to direct some of the great plays with the best actors in the country. I call my time in Adelaide as his collaborator my Golden Years. There I was, directing classics like Shakespeare's *King Lear* on the main stage with John Gaden as Lear, Geoffrey Rush as The Fool, John Howard as Edmond and Geoff Morrell as Edgar — a dream cast!

By the time I left the South Australian Theatre Company, I was a proven director. It was quite a unique path; not that there is any one particular path, everybody's path is different in the theatre — and luck and chance have something to do with it too. I was very fortunate to have gone from NIDA to being the associate director of a State theatre company, and especially having a string of classical plays on my CV by the time I was 30.

I could have stayed in Adelaide as the new artistic director, after John Gaden left, but I felt like our very special and unique collaboration had been the main reason for being there. So I too moved on. I spent two years as associate director to Roger Hodgman at the Melbourne Theatre Company and a year with George Miller (another generous teacher and mentor) in America on the film *Lorenzo's Oil.* Then I worked as a freelance director whose diary was, thankfully, always full. I did not plan ahead much, I just went where the opportunities presented themselves. I certainly did not intend to have an overseas career — it just happened, and I ended up staying away for 10 years.

In the mid-1980s, the English director Trevor Nunn was coming to Australia to remount *Les Misérables* and was looking for someone to work with him. In theatre circles, Trevor Nunn was a god, and his production of *Les Misérables* in England went on to become one of the great musical productions of the twentieth century. I got a call out of the blue and, after an interview, was offered the job as Trevor's associate director on the Australian production. I was astounded and thrilled, except at the time I had no idea what the show was. I went out and bought the CD. In 1984 news of *Les Misérables* was yet to hit Australia. Anyway, four days later James Thane and John Robertson gave me the job, and I was on a plane to New York for eight weeks where Trevor was directing *Les Misérables* on Broadway. I didn't know it at the time, but it was an indication of the lunatic spontaneity which was about to drive my life for a decade.

Trevor came to Australia the following year and, in the absence of his co-director John Caird, we did the show together. I then looked after it for five years, recasting it and redirecting it in various major cities around Australia. I loved the show and all the lessons I had learnt from Trev. He became a great mentor and supporter. Here was a great director who moved easily between the classics (he ran the Royal Shakespeare Company for 20 years) and musicals, and invested musical theatre with a dignity and importance. His process in the rehearsal room for a musical was as in-depth and investigative and challenging as if he was directing a Shakespeare play.

No director in Australia had ever had a career such as Trevor Nunn's and here I was apprenticed to one of the greats. There is no doubt that working with Trevor Nunn had a profound effect on my view of directing and my career aims. He was the reason why I got the job directing *Les Misérables* in Vienna a year later, by myself, and in *German*! I became his deputy. He was the first person to suggest that I go to London, even though I didn't take him seriously at the time. It wasn't until I directed Andrew Lloyd Webber's *Aspects of Love* in Sydney, many years later, that I finally did leave Australia for England.

I'm often asked if I see myself as ambitious, but really, when it comes down to it, most of the pivotal experiences in my career, I mean those that shaped its direction, have happened by chance, not because I had a grand plan or strategy, contrary to what some people may think. I didn't wake up one day and say, 'I'm going to be a theatre director and I'm going to Broadway and the West End.' I had no mythology about Broadway. To a degree, I did have fantasies about England because I saw Europe as a place of artistic inspiration, because of its architecture, its history, its various countries squashed together in such close proximity, its art. But I never saw Broadway as an inspiring place.

When the word ambition is attached to successful women, it's usually used as a negative. It implies a degree of aggressiveness and calculation, that you're an 'upwardly mobile' person looking for your next opportunity, your next stepping stone, regardless of who gets in the way. I was never like that. I rarely planned anything. I may have been driven and obsessive about my work because I loved it and breathed it. I did put enormous expectations on myself. I wanted to create great events for audiences in theatres, I believed in the importance of theatre to our daily lives and to our cultural identity. And I wanted to be good and to be taken seriously. But I don't call any of those things being ambitious in the negative sense.

The opportunity to direct in London, which led me to Broadway, came about purely by chance. I was in Sydney directing the Andrew Lloyd Webber musical *Aspects of Love.* It had failed in the West End and on Broadway earlier. You'd think that no one in their right mind would touch such a flop. James Thane had moved from the Australian office of the Cameron Mackintosh Organisation to the Australian office of the Really Useful

Company, and he had a dream that, with the right production, it could work. He invited me to direct it. At first, I remember thinking, 'Are you kidding? How can I make this work?' I listened to it and worked on the script and realised that it wasn't so bad, it had a lot of insightful things to say about love and the human condition. And its strength was the music — haunting and romantic. It was more like a Chekhov play than a blockbuster musical. I became passionate about solving its problems — I love a challenge. I used to call it my crippled child. I just had to see if it could walk.

In the end, the Australian production of *Aspects of Love* was very successful in Sydney. That was the end of it, I thought, except that the man who co-wrote the original lyrics, Don Black, happened to be in Australia on holiday from England and saw it. He rang Andrew Lloyd Webber in London and raved about it. 'You've got to come and see it. There's something really special happening here. Some woman called Gale Edwards has directed it,' Don told him.

Andrew flew out to Australia, saw the show and rang me at midnight the same night: 'I am moved, I'm sobbing. You've seen into the heart of my work. It's a wonderful production. I want you to work with me.' I couldn't believe it. I had never met Andrew Lloyd Webber. I had no idea Don Black had seen it or that Andrew, of all people, was in the audience that night. And so fate stepped in again.

He took me back to London with him to redirect

Aspects of Love with an English cast and we toured it all over England for two years, until it landed on the West End for the second time. Because the musical had been a critical failure before, Andrew was determined to prove that he could make a success of it. And we did it. It received great reviews, mainly for its simplicity of style and human perspective. Andrew was pleased and my life was changed.

After *Aspects of Love* I stayed on in London and worked with Andrew for another seven years, while also being invited into other English institutions as well. I worked at the English National Opera, the Royal Shakespeare Company (four times) and the Chichester Festival as well as directing George Bernard Shaw's *Saint Joan* on the West End. All the while I was collaborating with Andrew on his next project, *Whistle Down The Wind,* and directing a serious and epic version of *Jesus Christ Superstar* for the West End.

Now, Andrew is probably the most famous and most prolific composer of the late twentieth century. He is, in my opinion, a genius. He is also notorious for many things: for being difficult and demanding, and he is probably all of that and more — but I got along very well with him. I think this was partly because I am a woman (the first female director Andrew had ever employed). Andrew likes women and he has a very different relationship with women to what he does with men. I think my Australianness also helped; I think he found it refreshing. Anyway, we enjoyed a great collaboration for a long time. *Whistle Down the Wind* ran on the West End for three years and I directed two different versions of *Jesus Christ Superstar*, both critically acclaimed, which toured England and Europe, and later went to Broadway.

They were thrilling, tough, confronting, challenging and adventurous years. I was travelling constantly, sometimes back to Australia to direct here as well. I did *Saint Joan* (with an Australian cast), *Arcadia* and *The Boy From Oz* (four years in the making from the first meetings and workshops to opening night) in Sydney during those years.

I was mainly flying between America and London or around Europe. There was no time for a personal life. I was on an incredible schedule, always planning, casting, and designing the next show while directing the current one and often in two different countries. It was a roller-coaster ride. The pressure was immense because the stakes were so high. And people's behaviour is affected when millions of dollars are at stake. They aren't always nice and calm to deal with. There were times when I felt like I was living inside a mental asylum. And other times when I felt like the luckiest girl in the world.

In 1999 I went to Broadway with the production of *Jesus Christ Superstar* that had been acclaimed in England

and Europe. It was a dark interpretation of the show — no dancing in bell-bottom pants — I did it like a great epic play about the suffering of one extraordinary individual. We set it in war torn ruins and dressed the actors in contemporary costumes. Everything went well until late in the preview period when the producers and I disagreed about firing a key cast member. I felt that the firing was detrimental to the show, to the ensemble morale and to my own position as director, so I fought the decision.

And lost. It was a week to opening night, a critical time to unhinge the production. A few days later, with the show now unstable and, in my opinion, less than it should have been, the critics came in. The reviews panned the production that had been an unqualified success everywhere else, and Andrew took it off after four months.

Broadway is extremely tough. You have to be made of steel to survive. When you're in you're *in* and when you're out you're *out*. It's completely unforgiving. It has nothing to do with encouragement or development. It's about selling theatre to consumers and making money. It thrives only on success, not on art. When you arrive on Broadway as a new talent, there's a buzz of excitement because everyone is hoping that you will be able to deliver the big bucks. If you don't deliver, then very quickly everyone stops caring about what your view of art is or what you're aiming for. After the reviews came out, nobody rang.

Silence. The silence of failure.

Jesus Christ Superstar on Broadway was a bittersweet experience. It cost seven million dollars to make and it lost seven million dollars. It also ended my relationship with Andrew Lloyd Webber, and with some dear colleagues and collaborators who I had a long history with. The day the reviews came out the producers of *The Boy From Oz* rang and fired me and the entire creative team. This seemed so unfair as we had created *The Boy From Oz* from scratch. I was devastated. I remember lying in bed in an apartment in New York, my whole career collapsing around me.

This was probably my lowest point. And it was made worse by the fact that the *Sydney Morning Herald* printed excerpts from all the bad reviews, but never any of the raves I had received in London for other shows over the years, including the very same production of *Jesus Christ Superstar*. I was exhausted — mentally, emotionally and physically. After years of globetrotting and doing productions in high-focus places and high-stress situations, I was losing touch with what it was that I loved about the theatre. I was beginning to just *survive*. And Broadway taught me that even that was going to be tough.

Critics! Well … they are a whole other story. On Broadway and the West End the critics have enormous power. A bad review can literally close down a big commercial show, regardless of how popular it is with the audiences — before the critics get in there anyway. No one can afford the high prices for shows any more if a review says it's not good. Who can afford to take the risk for US$200?

I try not to put a lot of stock in the critics any more. I remember times when I've sat on the floor and sobbed while reviews tearing my work to pieces came off my fax machine. It always feels like they are tearing *you* to pieces, and sometimes they are. Once or twice in my career I've felt so destroyed that I thought I would never get up and walk again, let alone *work* again. Now I am grown up enough to have a policy of not reading them. *Any* of them. Not the good ones or the bad ones. That takes its own kind of strength, to become the critic of your own work. I know when I've done something really special, or when the work is compromised for whatever reason. I try to bring that objectivity to it, after opening night, when I can return to a show and just sit in the back row and look at it, without stress. I try to evaluate it dispassionately, to enjoy it and to analyse it as if I didn't do it. I prefer this system to rushing out in the morning to read what some guy has written about you in the paper, when half the time his credentials and his politics are seriously in question anyway.

But it's not just the critics that make the life of a theatre director tricky sometimes. Directing is a tremendously difficult occupation for so many reasons.

It's incredibly competitive, and while you're surrounded by people all of the time, essentially you are very alone. I've directed lots of big musicals and operas, I've worked on productions with 100 people working for me, but the director is always somehow isolated because the buck stops with you. You can't come in and say, 'I feel sick today, I don't feel like working' or 'I'm a bit down today because my boyfriend or girlfriend left me.' No one's interested. You are there to serve the work, to drive the ship, to inspire and guide the actors, to bring a vision to life, to satisfy the producers, to lead the creative team and to be true to your interpretation of a writer's work. It is a strangely isolated job in an intensely public arena.

You're also the conduit that joins the production to the management, so if there's any hostility from the producers about a particular issue, an actor or whatever, you have to be the buffer that filters it. You're the person negotiating with the producers, and if it's on Broadway or the West End, we're talking about millions and millions of dollars. We're talking about producers who are terrified of losing money, producers who are bullies, or have a power problem or are misogynistic or just downright loony. And believe me, I've worked with them all. The director has to absorb all of that and keep going as if there's no problem at all, so that everyone else feels secure and can keep being productive. And sometimes that means being locked in a room and having a difficult debate (or being shouted at) way into the night after 16-hour days, after everyone else has gone home, and still turning up early the next morning and not letting on that there's a problem.

You can never let the actors know about those things because they need to work from a place of security and innocence to be able to give you their best. Involving them in behind-closed-doors politics will destroy that. And on top of all that, you have to make everybody else feel special and important. Then, of course, all you've got to do is get the whole thing up on stage and make it work!

During breaks in the day, actors often go into the green room and sit around with a coffee and share their insecurities, their excitements and the gossip. Where does the director go? Usually into your office where the producer is waiting to ask you a million questions, the costume designer wants your opinion on a wig, the lighting designer wants a meeting, the assistant director wants tomorrow's schedule, and the stage manager has a prop problem. It is just relentless.

Of course, you work so intensely with the same people every day that you do tend to become quite close, especially with the actors. You are their colleague and there can be great love, respect and closeness between you but in the end you are the captain of the ship and friendship messes with your sense of authority. You can't sit around in the green room sharing your intimate stories and airing your dirty laundry because once the break is over you'll all be back in the rehearsal room and you might have to say, 'No, I don't want you to play it like that, I want it like this.'

The actors also have to learn to bond together without you because after opening night the director's job is over and they will have to carry the show together on their own. So often opening night would come and the actors would be feeling fabulous because they were finally out on stage in front of the audience, releasing all of their adrenaline, and getting applause. I'd be sitting in the stalls feeling tense, willing it to go right, feeling powerless to do anything if it didn't. The show would end to a standing ovation but by the time it was all over I'd be so exhausted that I would get through part of the opening night party and go home early to bed — alone. I'm talking about the *big* shows, thankfully it's not always that intense. It would kill you if it was.

I was doing very big gigs like that for a long time in my life, one after the other, and after every opening night I would go home feeling like I had just lost something. Then, for the next three or four days I would have all the signs of somebody going through grief. I'd be depressed and irritable and I'd feel aimless. After weeks and weeks of working so intensely, it would all be over in one night and that would be the last I'd have to do with it. Mostly, I had no time to deal with how I was feeling because, within a few days, I was usually on a plane to another State or country to start working on the next show. It wasn't a healthy way to live. But I was working on the international landscape in the most brutal genre there is — commercial musicals.

You need phenomenal stamina and an iron will to sustain a life like that. You really need a spine of steel to survive the international commercial world where producers like Andrew Lloyd Webber, Cameron Mackintosh and Robert Stigwood are calling the shots and big money is involved. And I enjoyed a very privileged position in that world for nearly a decade. I am quite proud of my achievements, and I don't regret any of it. I got to work with extremely talented people who became colleagues and friends, I had fabulous experiences in exotic locations and wined and dined with the most interesting and gifted people alive in the world of theatre. And I was constantly challenged as an artist and required to push the boundaries out further and further. I certainly became a more skilled director.

But the downside was that I had no personal life at all. I was always too busy, literally running from job to job. As a director, you're always designing and conceptualising the next show while you're in the middle of directing the current one. You've got to do it that way in order to make a living because, contrary to what many people believe, theatre directors don't actually get paid that much money. Unless of course you do huge musicals, but even then there's no guarantee because the royalty structures these days are very punitive. On paper, it's easy for clever accountants to turn what you thought was a successful musical into a venture that made a loss rather than a profit, which effectively shrinks your royalty rate. The era of becoming a millionaire out of musicals is over.

I was at a stage in my life where my work and my personal identity became indivisible. In fact the only Gale Edwards that existed was the theatre director. I was moving about the world with such velocity that the old friends I did have in Australia thought I was too busy leading this incredibly glamorous and successful international life to bother with them. 'She's working with Andrew Lloyd Webber on the West End ... She's directing at the Royal Shakespeare Company in England ...' That's what it looked like, and on one level it was. Success was all of the things I hoped it would be — amazing, sensational and challenging. But it was also wearying and lonely and those two things became heavy weights to bear as the years went on. And, frankly, I missed home. I missed Australia.

Two years ago, on Broadway, it finally came to an end. I was 45 years old and I knew I couldn't sustain that lifestyle any longer. There had to be more to life and, for the first time ever, I was ready to find out. I came back to Australia and moved into the house in Sydney I'd bought as an investment a long time ago. The house had been badly neglected by all of the tenants it saw over the years. It was virtually falling down around me. But it was 'home'.

I remember thinking, I have this fantastic string of credits and I've done wonderful things that I'm terribly proud of, and some things that I'm not at all proud of. Some things that have broken my heart and some things that have made me feel fantastic. But, ultimately, who am I? There was no me.

I'm envious of the 'Super Woman' who can do all this and have a husband and kids as well — a support structure. I think I really missed that. I just never managed to make that happen. I was also a woman working in a male-dominated world and when I was establishing my career women directors were given few opportunities, so if you fucked up you didn't get another job. My perception of it was that where the boys were allowed to fuck up time and time again, and were still encouraged and got another job, the girls would be cut off the dance card list if they failed just once. So I did feel enormous pressure to be as good as the best of the boys — consistently.

I was young and had masses of energy and enthusiasm and I was in love with the theatre. I wanted the next challenge. And I believed the theatre was important. I wanted to have a career like Richard Wherrett or Neil Armfield, and later Trevor Nunn. They were my mentors and I wanted to be like them. I never stopped to consider, or even notice, the sacrifices I was making.

It seemed to me that as a woman, I certainly had to put my energy in very particular places in order to achieve that and I couldn't let myself fall below a certain standard. But the problem with that is, as an artist, you can't always succeed. And the higher you fly, the more likely it is that you have to take the fall, once in a while. That's how you learn and develop. It's like being a circus act — you lose your balance and fall, then you get up and try again, with a few bruises but a little more knowledge next time.

I've finally realised that. You're talking to someone who is clearly a lot older and wiser now. The theatre scene is so different these days. Now you'll see three or four women's names on the program of any company every season. It's not the same pressure. Now it's a given, rather than a novelty, or one could argue an anomaly, as it was in my day.

I do regret the fact that I never had children but I know that I wouldn't have achieved what I have if I'd had to fulfil the roles of wife and mother as well. I got to this level in my career because I gave it 100 per cent focus. I lived it, I breathed it. Motherhood would not have allowed me to do that. Men, on the other hand, are somehow allowed to give their work that level of focus and have a family at the same time. Women, largely, can rarely get away with being so committed to a career and having a domestic life as well. I admire the few that have achieved that.

Having said that, I think things are starting to change. At the end of the twentieth century men started to take on more responsibility within families. And you're seeing more highly successful women who are supported by their husbands, who in some cases are taking on the role of primary carer of their children. There are those rare men who are prepared to be itinerant and travel around the world with their partner and carry their suitcases. But for that to happen, you have to be making a phenomenal salary to support you both. The only problem with that is, women tend not to earn such big bucks. Certainly not in my field, even at my level.

Men like that are still quite rare. And then, of course, as you get older, the marketplace for finding a partner becomes more and more restricted because we live in such an ageist society. Everywhere you turn popular culture supports youth and beauty. As women get older, they become more and more invisible in society, and more and more invisible to men. That is the truth. There are exceptions to that rule, of course; there are older women who are terribly attractive and older women who find the love of their life at 50, but generally, it's really tough for a single woman over 40.

Despite all of the above, I knew that coming home two years ago was the right thing to do. It was time to stop, to take stock; time to figure out how I was going to resurrect a life that I had neglected and ignored for 10 years. Time to decide what kind of life I actually wanted for myself.

I just shut the front door to my house, stayed inside and started to renovate the dilapidated old terrace. It's amazing how therapeutic it is to bash away at walls and repaint and redesign your living space. And plant a garden! It turns out that renovating was a good move for my personal life too. I needed someone to help out and I noticed that the guy who lived two doors down from me was a builder. I hired him and over time we became great friends. The fact that he had nothing to do with the theatre was incredibly refreshing. He knew nothing about Gale the theatre director. To him, I was just Gale the woman who lived up the street, that was it. It had been so long, forever maybe, since I'd had a friendship with someone I didn't meet through work.

Slowly our friendship turned into a love affair and slowly that love affair turned into a relationship. That was two years ago now and we have a wonderful life together. Finally, at 47 years of age, I'm experiencing a relationship again for the first time in a decade and a half.

My partner is such a calming influence in my life; we seem to balance each other. I'm a non-stop dynamo often working on overdrive, and he is slower-paced, gentler, more earthed. I still love the theatre and I haven't stopped working, but I enjoy the other side of my life too, and I'm certainly a much better person for it. And of course, having a relationship in this day and age has its own challenges, especially when your work takes you overseas constantly. It is virtually impossible to make a living in Australia as a freelance director in the theatre any more.

Altogether I spend about six months of the year away from home, but for the first time in my life I miss it, I miss the man who shares my life. When I go away for long periods we always make sure that he flies over to visit a few times, and always for opening night. I'll do whatever it takes to make sure that he is involved in my life. I can't just disappear for months on end like I used to. I've realised that real people in real relationships just can't live like that.

I'm so lucky to have found a man who is incredibly supportive of my work. He loves it! When he comes to the opening night of one of my shows you can see him just bursting with pride. He's so interested in learning about my world, which is quite rare, I think. Many men of his age feel threatened by a successful woman who has her own career. But he's got a lot to teach me too — about contentment and simplicity, about taking time to smell the flowers.

We often joke that I've still got my training wheels on. I'm still learning about all of this domestic, sharing-a-home-together stuff. It's incredible to be experiencing these things for the first time. He has an adorable 15-year-old son and he lives with us. Now having a child around is definitely something new to me! I can't believe that I'm finally learning about parenting after putting it on the back burner for so long. What a terrible tragedy it would have been for me to miss out on this in my life. For a long time there it did look as though it would never happen. It was a very desolate and depressing thought.

I've been on a tremendous journey, there's no doubt about that. It's become a cliché now, but while you can't control what happens to you in life, you can control how you respond to it. Even when things looked grim, I couldn't allow myself to become jaded and cynical or resigned, which is what I see in some people my age.

And I may go back there [to London] one day, but just at the moment, I'm quite happy to have found that balance in my life that allows me to be a woman, which I used to overlook as unimportant. I have a life now that allows me to be a partner, a lover, a wife, a friend, as well as a director. It's been thrilling to be able to define myself in new ways. There is no way I will stop being a director because it's what I am — it's in my soul, it's what I was born to be. It's what I love. But I now have another life as well. And that has been the best thing in the world for me.

jan chapman

jan chapman

Producer Jan Chapman is one of the pioneers of the modern Australian film industry. Along with her counterparts — many of them friends and collaborators — including directors Jane Campion, Gillian Armstrong, Peter Weir, Fred Schepisi, George Miller, Bruce Beresford and Phillip Noyce, Chapman helped shape the destiny of contemporary Australian film, laying the foundations for unprecedented international recognition of Australian writers, directors, producers and actors.

Before producing feature films, Chapman was behind some of the best of Australian television drama, including the ABC series *Sweet and Sour*, and the hugely successful miniseries *Come In Spinner.*

As an independent producer, *The Last Days of Chez Nous*, directed by Gillian Armstrong, marked Chapman's feature film debut. Since then, she has gone on to make some of Australia's most celebrated films, including the critically acclaimed *The Piano* with director Jane Campion, which won the coveted Palme d'Or at the Cannes Film Festival, three Academy Awards and 11 Australian Film Institute Awards.

More recently, Chapman produced the much lauded Ray Lawrence film *Lantana*, which screened to critical acclaim at film festivals around Australia and the world.

I've always had a fascination with storytelling. I was enamoured of art and literature when I was growing up. I was particularly interested in English literature. I was passionately nuts about it really. And storytelling. I love to tell a story, I love to work on refining the process of storytelling.

When I was in fifth class I moved from my primary school to an opportunity school, or what you would call a selective school now. It changed my life. I was a very shy, kind of unremarkable young girl who didn't have a high self-esteem and this school opened up a whole new world to me. The emphasis was very much on literature and music and the arts and my imagination was allowed to flourish. It was such a powerful thing for me. I loved it so much. I remember trying to write a book in fifth class. It was a kind of *Anne of Green Gables* written in an exercise book.

From here on, the desire to tell stories just took over, I never stopped thinking about it. I didn't dream of a career as such, but I did know that I wanted to tell stories. If you love books, you'll know what I mean. It just got me. I wouldn't say that I was ever particularly ambitious but I've always been driven. Driven to make films and tell stories, rather than to become a famous film producer or director.

In high school I had a wonderful, deeply inspiring English teacher who introduced me to poetry. It was just the most exciting thing in the whole world to me then. Actually, I don't think anything since has ever affected me as strongly, except perhaps for the birth of my son many years later when I was 40.

In my early twenties, I joined the Sydney Filmmakers Co-op, a group of independent filmmakers. It was one of the most defining experiences of my life, for so many reasons. It was where I met Phillip Noyce, who actually became my first husband, Peter Weir, and Gillian Armstrong, who became a lifelong friend and collaborator.

Phil and I were both still at university when we met. I was studying Fine Arts, English and Philosophy, and he had already started making films. We fell in love and ended up getting married when I was 21. To me, film was the most perfect medium for telling stories. There was an art element to it and it was great fun. Phil was incredibly obsessive about it. He became the manager of the Filmmakers Co-op and at one point we had the Co-op in our house. That was really mad. I can't remember exactly how it started but I think we got a grant so we could afford to hire an office and a few staff. We worked on each other's films and showed them in this little theatre in St Peters Lane in Darlinghurst that we had redecorated ourselves. Most of us were making short films from 15 minutes to 50 minutes. Film was everything to us. We worked, talked, thought and felt film. It hasn't changed that much actually, but as you get older you start to share that focus with other things in your life.

We'd go to the Sydney Film Festival and all be very inspired by the European films and some of the American independent films. There was a lot of exchanging of ideas between us and a lot of talk that went on. It was such a fertile, creative ground for a bunch of kids who had big dreams. It was really just a step up from childhood backyard performances, but so integral to our development as filmmakers. It was so hands-on and you really had that experience of an audience responding to a film.

It's funny because it seemed so easy then. If you wanted to make a film you'd just go out and do it. I never thought that anything would stop me from making films because I learnt early on that it was very possible, not only to make them but to actually have people see them.

I think that's partly why the Australian film industry is so strong. I mean, there were a couple of people who actually started it, who had a vision for an independent filmmaking community. Albie Thoms, who is now a director, was one of them and our little Filmmakers Co-op was almost like an embryonic prototype.

Film and media have become so popular. Now there are things like Tropfest, which has given young filmmakers a huge platform. When John Polson started Tropfest I thought it was amazing, it was just like what we were doing with the Co-op all those years ago. There wasn't much of a local film industry or a lot of government support when I started my career in the early 1970s, certainly nothing like it is now with organisations like the Film Finance Corporation. When I first started filmmakers only had each other for support. But it has become so huge now that I don't quite know where it fits in. It's still really great, but I think some people make their film just to be in Tropfest, rather than actually wanting to say something. Of course, there are a lot of exceptions. People like Gregor Jordan, who made his fabulous film *Two Hands* and has gone on to work in the industry overseas in a big way.

I look back now and realise that if I hadn't met Phil and been exposed to the film world, I may not have found an outlet for my passion for storytelling and creativity. I just loved the language of film, but it took me a while to work this out. I taught English and Arts for two years before I started working professionally in the television and film industry.

My marriage to Phil was full of making films. The first year the Australian Film, Television and Radio School opened, he and Gill Armstrong immediately applied and were accepted. On the day Phil went to put in his application I actually half-heartedly applied too, but I remember thinking that I shouldn't because film was his thing. At that stage I was still teaching and I felt that I would somehow be stepping on his toes if I went to film school as well.

When Phil and Gill finished their first year at film school they were sent to a film festival in France, so we went on a six-month trip around the world together. Seeing the world was amazing and it was then that I realised I didn't want to go back to teaching.

There's a strong film industry here but it's still hard to get a job. I was very lucky because I got my start at the ABC and that was incredibly important for me. Albie Thoms, who I'd met at the Sydney Filmmakers Co-op, helped me get my first job in television. It was the early 1970s and he was working on a show at the ABC called GTK. It was a 10-minute show of interviews with people involved in fashion, bands and film. Albie asked me to be an interviewer, which was kind of amusing seeing that I wasn't very knowledgeable about the pop world — I spent my childhood and teenage years with my head buried in the English classics. Anyway, one thing led to the other and I became a researcher in that department. When I joined I was trained in radio and television and then I moved into educational television before I went to the drama department. There was more of a possibility for a career path then.

When I meet film school students now, I wonder what they are going to do, how they'll find work. We're all constantly lobbying to keep up the requirements for the number of hours of Australian television, not only because it's important to have Australian drama amongst all of the foreign programming you see on the television, but also because it's a training ground for the next generation of filmmakers.

I worked at the ABC for 14 years before I became an independent producer. I was with the ABC at a time when I was fortunate enough to develop the material I liked — I had a lot of creative freedom. All the while I worked in television, I still worked on other people's films. That was my hobby all right. It was what I did in my spare time. Film was about self-expression to me. I've always seen it like that. I've never seen it as a commercially orientated thing.

I left there about the same time the Film Finance Corporation started, which has become so vital to the film industry. In fact, the first feature film I made as an independent producer, after I left the ABC, *The Last Days of Chez Nous* with Gillian Armstrong, was fully funded by the FFC. In those days, they used to choose three or four films a year and fully fund them.

Strangely, as I make more films, I'm starting to feel that the whole process is actually becoming harder, rather than easier. I think that's because I'm aware of the difficulties I'm likely to confront. You just know that there will be times when you feel as though you've hit a brick wall. The great thing about starting out is that you're still naive about the inevitable obstacles, and all you have are your hopes and dreams.

When you are making a film you are always hopeful that it will connect with audiences and you always plan for it to, but you never quite know how it's going to be received. I'm really pleased that my last film, *Lantana*, connected with Australian audiences so strongly, particularly because it was quite a small story and we had a mostly Australian cast. It's an exploration of adult relationships and marriage. It's not a quirky comedy like a lot of Australian films have been. It's a serious film and it is harder to get people to see serious films. It makes you feel that, as a culture, we are starting to feel confident about ourselves and ready to see our own stories on screen.

Making *Lantana* was quite a journey. When I was trying to sell the idea to distributors they were worried about how they could market it because it wasn't a high concept film or something they could easily describe in one line, even though they were all very attracted to the script and then to the finished film. It's almost impossible not to become deeply attached to the film you are making. As a producer, you are so involved in actually getting the film off the ground that you feel very responsible for it and the other people involved. Making films is such a long and consuming process — *Lantana* took three years to make, from the beginning of the script to the finished film. From the moment you decide to take a film on you know that it's going to be a major part of your life for a number of years. It will be completely present in your mind all of the time. And you know, as well as some exciting times, there will be disappointments you have to go through before it all works out in the end.

You work on scripts for such a long time that you can end up picking them to death, but spending all that time on them does mean that they get better, and so does your understanding of the story. Often I will develop two or three things at the one time. Once I did three films in three years, one after the other. It's not often that you spend a long time just developing; you're often developing and making something at the same time.

What's difficult, I suppose, is that I'm an independent producer, which means it's just me and an assistant until we start production on a film, when there can be up to a hundred people working with us. The great benefit of being independent means that you can do what you like, when you like, and after more than a decade, I don't think it would suit me to be any other way. But it does feel a bit lonely sometimes. A bit like you're it, everything is resting on your shoulders. That's quite hard.

Filmmaking is so consuming that you tend to really value the off times when you're in-between the most hectic parts of the process. I'm just about to start work on a new project but I feel like I'd like to stay on pause for a bit longer because I know that as soon as I start working on it, that will be it for my freedom of mind. Mentally, it will be there all the time. Working on the script and putting the film together is always enjoyable and deeply fulfilling for me, but always lurking in the back of my mind is the fact that I never really know whether the film will actually get made, at least in the early stages. That is difficult.

You do need a tremendous amount of perseverance and determination to get through the process and you can drive yourself crazy sometimes. The thing is, making films requires a lot of money — six to ten million Australian dollars or more — and people don't give that kind of money away lightly. I'm respectful of that. So it's really no wonder that it's not easy. Finding the right person, someone who really believes in the film and is also willing to sign the cheque, is quite a funny business.

Sometimes, when you're going along the usual track, visiting distributors and the people you believe are most likely to finance the film, something turns up from left of field. That has happened to me a couple of times. It happened with *The Piano*, which was financed by a French businessman who decided he wanted to finance 10 great filmmakers around the world. It was wonderful really. And with *Walk the Talk* we had David Geffen from Dreamworks behind us. Those sorts of magical things do come along sometimes.

Then there are times when it seems as though no one is going to come on board and you're so despondent that you feel like giving up. There was a time with *Lantana* when it looked like I wasn't going to be able to raise the money, even though I had explored all the possibilities. I couldn't work out why the people we approached weren't giving us the money when they kept telling us how much they liked it. It's interesting because when I'd finally resigned myself to defeat, the money did come through and it all finally came together. There's something to be said for surrendering control of things.

But unfortunately, it doesn't always work out that way. There is one project that I have just let go, but in the back of my mind I still think it will turn up again. You put so much time and so much of yourself into developing a project that it's incredibly sad to have to let it go just because of the lack of funding. And you feel so responsible for the other people involved. For that reason, because it is so heartbreaking, I don't allow that possibility to enter my mind very often.

It's funny the way things have worked out. Phil was absolutely passionate about film all the time we were married, whereas in those early years, I was only starting. I do think that the fact that my marriage split up when I was 27 gave me the space to develop without being under Phil's aura. He is a very strong personality. He is a fabulous person and I have great admiration for him, but it was hard to express myself when he was so prominent. I think it's hard for both people to be centre stage at once in a relationship. I don't know if it can work really.

I met my second husband, Stephen, at the ABC, where he was a line producer. He'd also been an actor for a long time. The way our marriage has developed, especially since we had our son, Jack, has meant that Stephen has taken on a lot of the household responsibilities. I don't mean that that's all he does, because he still works as an actor, but he does much more than his fair share of domestic things and he has always been happy to just pack up and move whenever we needed to go somewhere for my work. He left his job at the ABC to come to New Zealand with me when we did *The Piano* not long after we'd just had Jack. It is wonderful to have that kind of support, but on the other hand you do have to watch it. You can't let your lives revolve too much around one partner's career. The other person may well need to have their time in the limelight. I'm really lucky that Stephen loves show business and films. He belongs to that world too. Many of his friends are actors and film people.

I didn't have my son until I was 40. I honestly don't remember thinking about having children in my first marriage. But then again, I was only in my twenties. With Stephen, having a child was something I really wanted to do. I actually had a number of miscarriages, so becoming a mother happened a little later than I intended. That happens to so many women in their mid- and late-thirties, it is harder to have children. You don't think about it in your twenties and then by the time you are ready to do it you discover that falling pregnant is not the sort of thing you can just do on cue.

But it all worked out quite well for me. Having Jack was the beginning of a new chapter in my life. I'd just left the ABC after 14 years and I was working on *Chez Nous*, my first film as an independent producer. And then six months after Jack was born we went to New Zealand to make *The Piano*.

I absolutely adore my son. He is just a constant joy in my life — always amusing and interesting. I came to being a mother really wanting it, and I think that's because it happened a little later in life for me. Having Jack was an amazing, miraculous and extraordinary journey. After he was born I remember thinking, 'If only someone had told me how this feels, I would have done this a whole lot earlier and maybe had more kids.' Although, you realise that if you are going to work and live this kind of life, then it is hard to share it with a large family.

Even though I've had these two lines in my life, family and work, they've always been very intertwined. Having a family does help you keep things in perspective. Life wouldn't be nearly as interesting if I didn't have a child and husband to share it with.

I remember when we won the Palme d'Or at Cannes for *The Piano*. Stephen was sitting there with his older daughter from another marriage, and I remember thinking that the joy I felt wouldn't be the same if he wasn't right there to share it with me.

Having a family and career is hard, but it's also very invigorating and rewarding. But I know that if I hadn't had a partner like Stephen who has supported me, then my life wouldn't have been as fulfilling as it has been. Sometimes I underestimate how lucky I've been in that regard. I can't imagine doing this — running a business making films and raising a child — with somebody who had a whole other career in another world. That would be difficult.

In Australia, it seems that women have had a pretty good run. If you look at the number of female directors and producers who have done very well, it is a high percentage in comparison with other countries. Margaret Fink and Pat

Lovell were fantastic producers who were a little bit ahead of me. People like Gill [Armstrong] and Jane [Campion] are such great role models for young women today.

However, for all the presence of women in the film world, it is a worry when you think that it was only just under 10 years ago that Jane became the first woman ever to win the Palme d'Or at Cannes, and no woman has ever won best director for a feature film at the Academy Awards, not yet anyway.

I do think that it's still tough for women in some industries — certainly in politics and in business when you look at how few women hold really important roles. But I must admit that I've never felt that being a woman has been a problem. I think the situation in the film world in America is different. The Hollywood studio system, which is very hierarchical, is a lot like the business world and very much dominated by men. I think that's why it doesn't appeal to me. I've never really contemplated moving to America. The people I know who work there say the scripts they see are lacking in quality a lot of the time. The nature of my role as a producer means that I can do my job just about anywhere. But I am Australian and the stories I'm interested in telling come from here.

It's interesting how you feel when you do achieve a certain amount of success. *The Piano* took us on a remarkable ride, indeed, all the way to Hollywood. It was wonderful but there is a price you pay for it. You realise that winning awards and acclaim is not everything. Ultimately, personal happiness is the only thing that matters. If you're not happy within yourself, if you don't feel inner peace, then what other people think about your work doesn't matter.

But having said that, winning an Oscar was fabulous. The best thing about it was that it was shared between a group of us who were so personally committed to that film. Actually, my relationship with Jane Campion is probably one of my great achievements of working in the film industry. I just like her so much. I think she's such an interesting, challenging human being.

I remember on the night of the Oscars we stayed in a house in Los Angeles with our husbands and friends. There was all the normal Oscar-time hoopla going on in Hollywood but the mood in our house was very normal and light-hearted. Aside, of course, from the ordeal of getting dressed for the Oscars and feeling like you didn't look any good.

There were moments when I almost felt like wanting to go home because it felt so fake, but it was thrilling to meet the people whose work I'd admired so much over the years. It felt like we really were part of an international industry. I couldn't believe the way the Americans welcomed us and appreciated our work. There seemed to be absolutely no boundaries. No xenophobia.

We had a lot of fabulous times with *The Piano*. That kind of public recognition is very emotional and powerful. In Cannes, the whole theatre stood up and applauded when it was screened. Once again the whole lot of us were there together — Jane, Holly Hunter and Harvey Keitel, who are Jane's and my friends still, and our husbands. It was such a wonderful team.

That's one of the things I really like about making films. The process of creating something with a group of people and believing in something together. You get to know people in a much deeper way when you work with them so intently. When you work on scripts, analysing and exploring characters, you uncover really deep levels of understanding about other human beings and that is a really great experience. It is so different to talking to people in a social sense. When you're working so closely you end up becoming a kind of family and you form relationships that last. I have a lot of friendships that have begun like that, as work, and have gone on for years and years.

After all this time, thinking about films and watching films is still one of the most enjoyable things in my life. Yesterday I watched *Monster's Ball.* It wasn't perfect but I loved watching it and it made me think that I'd rather be watching and thinking about films than just about anything else. Recently, a friend of mine told me that I needed a hobby. He was quite serious. I thought, well, film is my hobby. If I wasn't making films for a living, I would still be watching them, thinking about them and talking about them.

kirsty sword gusmao

kirsty sword gusmao

Before the rest of the world acknowledged the shocking human rights abuses in East Timor under Indonesian rule, a Melbourne woman named Kirsty Sword became intimately involved in East Timor's struggle for independence.

Working as an English teacher in Jakarta in the early 1990s, Sword became an undercover agent for the East Timorese Resistance movement, which was, to say the least, a dangerous undertaking. Anyone suspected of even supporting the Resistance, let alone being directly involved, could expect to be thrown into gaol or even executed.

Sword's involvement escalated when she began smuggling information to and from the Indonesian prison where the Resistance leader, Xanana Gusmao, was serving a life sentence after fighting the oppressive Indonesian military for 17 years in the mountains of East Timor.

What followed was one of the greatest and hard-won political and humanitarian triumphs of recent history — East Timor was granted independence — and also one of the greatest love stories. Through their correspondence, Sword and Gusmao fell in love, and maintained an intense relationship despite the fact that they only saw each other twice in the first four years while Gusmao was still imprisoned.

When Gusmao was finally released in 1999, they were married and Sword gave birth to their first child. In April 2002 Xanana Gusmao became the first democratically elected president of East Timor since Indonesian rule and Kirsty Sword Gusmao is now the country's First Lady. She lives in Dili with Gusmao and their son Alexandre and at the time of going to print was expecting their second child.

I grew up in Melbourne but my interest in Indonesia started when I was a child. When I was three or four years old my father went back to university and took Indonesian Studies. He would come home and teach my brother and me a few words of Indonesian and it didn't take long before we were running around the house saying 'selamat pagi' (good morning) and 'baik-baik saja' (just fine).

I studied Indonesian all through high school and went on to major in Indonesian Studies at Melbourne University, along with Italian. I learnt a lot about Indonesian politics there and more at the Indonesian department at Monash University, which was a much more dynamic, progressive institution. While I was at university, I got involved with a magazine published out of Melbourne called *Inside Indonesia*. It provided commentary and analyses on Indonesian socio-political life, and I did some editorial and administrative work for the magazine while I finished my studies.

I started travelling to Indonesia not long after that, in my early twenties. The first time I went was in 1984. I was enchanted by Indonesia and at that stage I knew little about the political repression and violation of human rights going on in places like East Timor. By my second or third visit, I'd made contact with Indonesian dissidents and East Timorese refugees in Australia through my work with the magazine, so when I arrived in Indonesia I already had a network of contacts. In Indonesia, I met more dissidents and refugees so I began looking behind the scenes at what was really going on. I continued to really love Indonesia and the Indonesian people, but started to delve into the politics a little more deeply.

I read up on the history of Indonesia's relationship with East Timor and by the time I began work on the English documentary *Cold Blood* — which helped in turning the tide against Indonesia by exposing some of what was really going on — I was well and truly involved. Because of my knowledge of Indonesian politics and the fact that I was fluent in the language, I was hired by the documentary makers to travel with them to Timor as a researcher and translator.

That was in 1991, more than 10 years ago now. It was my second trip to East Timor. I remember taking a three-week crash course in Portuguese before my first visit in 1990 so I would be able to communicate with the older Timorese who still spoke the language, even though Indonesian had been the official language since Indonesia invaded the country in 1975.

In 1991 in East Timor, things were reaching a breaking point. The Independence movement was preparing for the visit to Timor of a Portuguese parliamentary delegation and the Indonesian military was merciless in its reprisals against anyone suspected of wishing to meet and speak with the delegation. We interviewed a wide range of individuals, from students to members of the clergy, involved in some capacity in the clandestine movement. We captured a good deal of footage on daily life inside East Timor, the difficulties faced by all those who dared to speak out against the rampant human rights abuses, the fear and intimidation.

In November that year, not long after we left, news broke of the Santa Cruz cemetery massacre where hundreds of East Timorese were murdered by the Indonesian military during a peaceful and orderly funeral procession. I was in England at the time, working on post-production of the documentary. I was transcribing interviews and I realised that many of the people we'd spoken to were among those killed in the massacre. That affected me very deeply because amongst those that were gunned down on that day were young people who were virtually the only remaining members of their families, people with such commitment and loyalty to the ideal of independence and a better life for their fellow East Timorese.

After that experience I knew I wanted to do something to help. Not just campaign work in Australia, but something serious, real and concrete. A year later, when I was 26 years old, I moved to Jakarta to work as an English language consultant and trainer. I taught English to corporate workers — people in banks and large companies.

As well as teaching English, I did some voluntary work for a human rights organisation which had a specific focus on East Timor. Over time, my human rights work started to consume more and more of my energy. That was really the beginning of this kind of double life I ended up living. Officially I was an English teacher, but most of my energy was focused on the situation in East Timor. Eventually my involvement became more serious when I started working directly for the East Timorese Resistance, which, out of necessity, was a completely clandestine movement. The Indonesian military came down heavily on anyone suspected of supporting the Resistance movement and those found to be actively involved wound up in gaol subjected to torture or, in many cases, dead.

I first made contact with the Resistance when I was in East Timor working on the documentary. We interviewed some of the key figures and I stayed in touch with some of them. I was also still in contact with the East Timorese students and refugees I'd met in Jakarta, some of whom were also involved in the Resistance.

The Indonesian Government was militant in its efforts to cover up and downplay what was happening in East Timor, especially in terms of human rights abuses. The only hope for dissidents and people involved in the Resistance was to continue to alert the international community, human rights organisations and the media to the systematic terror and violence the Indonesian military was inflicting on the people.

Initially, I was involved in gathering information about human rights abuses, mostly from the East Timorese students I'd met in Jakarta. Many of them had experienced violation themselves and their own efforts to speak out by contacting human rights organisations or the media had landed them in trouble.

Many of these people became my friends. They grew to trust me and because I had access to secure communications — things like encrypted e-mail — I became a conduit for the information they were desperately trying to impart. An informal communication network developed where people would ring me and pass on information. News of what I was doing spread and eventually a whole series of people that I didn't know before, referred to me by their friends, were suddenly appearing and opening up, wanting to entrust information or documents to me.

There were plenty of spies and informants working for the Indonesian Intelligence so there was always potential for treachery. As a consequence, the issue of trust worked both ways. Whenever I was approached by someone I didn't know, I was always aware that they could be informants.

People built up their trust in me over time. I guess there weren't many other options available to them as there weren't many people in my position who were willing to help. But once I'd made contact with Xanana and it became evident to people that I had his trust, it was enough to signal to them that I was okay.

There was so much to be done. Sometimes it was as simple as providing financial assistance to Timorese students who'd had their scholarships cut off because they were involved in the Resistance or human rights work. Often they needed money to buy a ticket out of the country for their own safety, other times they needed to get back into East Timor to carry out important tasks for the Resistance.

Mostly I had to use my own money but sometimes I managed to scrape together enough amongst friends from the solidarity movement. Of course, I couldn't go around publicising what I was doing too widely. I certainly couldn't organise a fundraising dinner. It all had to be handled rather discreetly.

On a few occasions delegations from the United Nations and human rights organisations would visit Jakarta. Obviously, the Timorese students were extremely eager to make contact with them, even just to make a statement or pass on a report on what was happening in East Timor, but there was no way they could actually front up to a five-star hotel themselves and request an audience. They would have been arrested on the spot by one of the scores of military Intelligence officers who were always milling around the hotels, ready to pounce on any person attempting to approach a delegate.

That was where I could help. As a white Western woman I could easily slip through the radar. I'd get all dolled up and walk straight into those hotels, looking like I was part of the scene, and go straight to a delegate's room and knock on the door without being noticed. Often foreign delegates were accompanied by Indonesian military officers, which made things much harder.

On one occasion in 1994 I attempted to make contact with a visiting UN Special Rapporteur who was looking into the human rights situation in East Timor. I remember fronting up at his hotel with a statement. I thought this would be one of the easier ones to pull off because I'd been able to ring him beforehand and let him know I was coming without giving out too much information. I was always very aware of my phone being tapped.

When I arrived he was just about to head off to a big gala dinner and his hotel suite was teeming with Intelligence officers, speaking into walkie-talkies, who had been assigned to chauffeur him there. The delegate knew I was up to something but he didn't let on. He was a really cluey guy, he'd been to East Timor and he was very aware of what was really happening.

He called me into the bedroom and while he put his socks on, he said in a hushed voice, 'Okay, give me the documents' and I slipped them to him without being noticed. There was no way I could be seen to be passing documents to him — the Intelligence would have seized them immediately. My cover would have been blown and, at the least, I would have been deported.

I first came into contact with Xanana when friends from a Portuguese solidarity group asked for my help in conveying a message to him at Cipinang Prison, Jakarta, where he had been held since 1993. The Resistance still looked to Xanana for leadership, even though he was in prison serving what was at that stage still a life sentence. In this particular case, the group wanted his opinion on a lobbying strategy they were working on. They knew that I was living in Jakarta, that I had access to safe communication and a fairly broad network of East Timorese friends, many of whom, by then, were either visiting Xanana in gaol or were able to smuggle things to him through the prison guards who they paid to keep quiet. It was an informal but very well organised courier system which spanned from East Timor all the way to Jakarta and in and out of Cipinang Prison. It was quite amazing really.

I was good friends with another inmate at Cipinang, a political prisoner called Joao Freitas da Camara. He was arrested for organising a peaceful demonstration in Jakarta and protesting against the Santa Cruz massacre, and because he was the spokesperson for the demonstrators, was singled out and given a 10-year sentence. I had been writing to him since I moved to Jakarta. It was through Joao that I first made contact with Xanana.

It was very difficult in the beginning. Xanana was kept in virtual seclusion when he was moved to Cipinang. It was six months before Joao had enough regular contact with Xanana to tell him about me — this sympathetic foreigner in Jakarta who was willing to traffic information to and from the prison for the Resistance.

I started sending Xanana my greetings through Joao and he started writing to me. Initially it started quite innocently. One of the first things he asked me to do was send him some acrylic paints. He had some canvases and wanted to do some painting to help him pass the time.

Later he asked me to alert a friend of his from a human rights organisation in Portugal about what was going on in the gaol. When he was first moved to Cipinang he was being intimidated by other prisoners who were acting at the instigation of the military Intelligence. They would threaten and insult him to the point that their rantings would keep him awake all night. They were trying to break his spirit and literally drive him crazy. The military was a pretty constant presence at the prison when Xanana was first moved there and they were deliberately making life difficult for him.

Once I received a response from Xanana's friend in Portugal, I'd report back to him, then he would ask me to send his response and so on. Slowly, people in the Resistance and organisations sympathetic to the Resistance came to know that I was in contact with Xanana. Word of mouth spread and suddenly I was being contacted by people I didn't even know asking me to convey messages to him.

At first I used my contacts to smuggle documents and letters in to him but eventually I started going to the prison and paying off the guards myself. Later, I even managed to smuggle a mobile phone and a video camera into the prison. Xanana may have been incarcerated but he was still able to communicate with the outside world and continued to run the Resistance from his gaol cell.

My relationship with Xanana grew from there. We built up a relationship through our letters and a sense of trust developed between us. I reminded him that we almost met on one occasion a year before he was captured when I was in East Timor in 1991 working on the documentary. We'd planned to interview him but it was cancelled at the last minute when the meeting was deemed too dangerous. Over time, our contact became more regular. As he began to trust me more the things he asked me to do became more and more onerous.

But it wasn't all cloak and dagger stuff. Not long after we started writing I started teaching him English, kind of by correspondence. I was an English teacher so I had access to a lot of material. I would send him exercises photocopied from textbooks, he would complete them, send them back to me and I would correct them. Xanana has a really good sense of humour. He was always saying funny or provocative little things in his homework. We came to learn a lot about each other through those letters.

I remember sending him a photo because he had no idea what I looked like. It was actually a photo taken of the back of my head as I gazed out over emerald green rice paddies. I couldn't send him a photo of my face in case the letter was intercepted and I would be recognised. He did a painting of that photo, which I have always treasured and which now hangs over the bed in our bedroom.

In the end we wrote to each other virtually every day and then when he had the mobile phone we were making calls to each other backwards and forwards all the time. It was easy to develop a friendship with Xanana. He has a really warm, open and very spontaneous nature. Anyone that comes into contact with him is immediately taken by him. He is just so gregarious and genuinely interested in people.

We managed to find a common ground even though we came from different worlds and our lives were so opposite. I was from a middle-class family in Melbourne and he grew up in East Timor and had spent a large part of his life — 17 years — fighting in the hills and leading the Resistance. But if you stripped away all of the details we did have one thing in common. Essentially, we were two foreigners with uncertain futures living in this big, hostile city.

I think Xanana found comfort in the fact that there was someone out there who supported him. Our contact also allowed him to continue in his role as commander of the Resistance — he was still issuing orders and his fighters were obeying them. He continued to feel that he was a useful part of the command structure. In many ways I became his link to the outside world.

Before long a strong sense of solidarity developed between us. I guess it was the combination of gratitude that he felt for what I was doing and concern for the danger that he was putting me in. About six months after we started writing I met up with my family in Ambon for a holiday. My family knew that I was working for the Resistance and they knew that something was going on between Xanana and I. They were always really supportive of my involvement but there were times when they were seriously concerned for my safety, usually when they hadn't heard from me for a while. Anyway, when I got back from Ambon to my house in Jakarta there was a bagful of mail from Xanana waiting for me. I'd been away for three weeks but he continued to write every day. His letters were full of 'When are you coming back?' and 'I miss you'. I was so overwhelmed by his outpouring. We wrote to each other for nine months before we actually met and by then we had already acknowledged we had strong feelings for each other that had developed way beyond friendship.

Our first meeting was meticulously planned. Visitors were rarely allowed into the prison. Initially I was going to try to get in with a church group — many of whom were activists and using the group as a cover — who were granted limited, one-off access to the prison. I begged and pleaded with them to be included in their group but they didn't offer me any guarantees. 'Come along, if you get in you get in, if not, there's nothing we can do to help you,' they said. I decided that it was too much of a risk, so I waited for another opportunity which did present itself four months later in December.

There was one other exception to the no visitors rule — Christmas. It was the one day of the year when inmates were allowed to invite a friend or relative into the prison to celebrate the occasion. It was too dangerous for me to be linked to Xanana so I had to find another person in the prison to visit.

At the time there was an Australian man in the prison called John who Xanana had befriended, so we came up with a plan for me to visit pretending to be his niece.

We were so anxious about being caught, and we thought of everything that could possibly go wrong. All of the details were meticulously worked out; I even had a basket of apples for 'Uncle John', and I knew exactly where Xanana and John would be standing when we walked into the hall where we were allowed to sit down with the inmates for a communal Christmas lunch. When we finally did make it in, I had to give this guy John, my long lost uncle I'd never met in my life, a big hug. I shook Xanana's hand very formally and pretended not to notice him. It was completely bizarre.

We were elated to finally be in each other's presence but that was tempered by the circumstances. We had to be rather circumspect, which was very difficult seeing that this was our first real meeting after months and months of developing a relationship and falling in love through letters. We could hardly talk to one another so as not to arouse any suspicion.

I knew some of the other inmates as well, people who were imprisoned for meagre crimes such as participating in peaceful demonstrations against human rights abuses. My old friend Joao was there and so was another

Timorese guy I knew who was gaoled for a similarly inane 'crime'. It was an amazing reunion with old friends.

It was so exciting to finally be in the same room as Xanana. Just to be able to sit next to one another! The guards more or less allowed the inmates and their guests to enjoy themselves. We drew quite a bit of attention to ourselves in the end. We were sitting in a big group, laughing and talking and taking photos and clowning around. I never saw the photos from that day though — the guy who brought his camera along had it seized by guards as we left.

That was December 1994 and Xanana and I didn't see each other for another four years, until August 1998 when the rules governing access to Xanana were relaxed somewhat, thanks to the fall of President Suharto and the new era of 'reformasi' or reform. I tried numerous times to see him again after that first meeting, but I could not persuade the prison guards to let me in, no matter what I tried.

Xanana and I continued our relationship, despite the fact that it was impossible for us to see each other. For much of that time too, I had no idea whether he would ever actually be released. Even when his life sentence was reduced to 20 years, I knew it would be a long wait before we could be together.

Xanana felt incredibly guilty about our relationship. In his eyes I was this young person, 28 years old, who had her whole life ahead of her, and everything to lose by committing herself to a man who at best might not be free to be with her for another 20 years. To relieve the anxiety we used to joke about that a lot, how he would be old and grey and in a wheelchair by the time he was released. But more seriously, we had many fantasies and dreams about the life we would have together in East Timor. I guess that kept us both going.

We were both still aware that our love was very much untested, though. At least on my part there was always a reservation about whether our relationship could survive in the 'real' world. I'd been in relationships before and I knew all about the challenges of living with another human being on a day-to-day basis. Ironically, I probably had a lot more experience in relationships than Xanana even though he was 20 years older than me. He married and had children in his twenties but from the age of 28 he was a guerilla commander living in the jungle. That was virtually the end of his emotional life. In the back of my mind I was always thinking, 'Well, this is great but it has to be put to the reality test.' And at that stage, I had absolutely no idea when we might be in a position to do that, which made things even more difficult.

I had several periods of doubt over those years before Xanana was released, when the political situation did a complete turnaround and East Timor was granted independence. It was such a huge commitment to make, but after a couple of years things had reached such a level of intensity between us that it would have been hard for me to back out of the relationship, even if I wanted to.

One of the reasons was because my relationship with Xanana and my connection with East Timor's independence struggle had become so interlinked. From the beginning, my bond with Xanana was tied up with my commitment to the struggle. Part of my love and respect for him was a result of the position he took as political leader. Initially I was concerned that maybe I was in love with the myth of Xanana, but after a while I came to know so much about him that I could view his political persona as separate to his private one.

Dealing with our relationship was also difficult for Xanana. He is the type of person who lives life to the full and he was like a caged lion in that prison. He'd gone from leading the Resistance in the jungle to a life confined in a cell with virtually no access to normal human relationships. He was completely distanced from real life and I think our relationship was a lifeline to him.

Sometimes I felt like he was living his life vicariously through me. I know it sounds ridiculous, because we'd spent very little time physically being together, but there were times when I felt overwhelmed by his presence in my life. Often I felt like I was unable to do anything outside his sphere of influence. In many ways a relationship conducted over the phone and through letters wasn't enough, but somehow Xanana was a constant presence in my life and our relationship was intense most of the time.

But in a lot of ways we were just like a normal couple. We would discuss things into the early hours of the morning over the phone. We would have arguments about things, lovers' quarrels. Once he wouldn't ring me for two days because he was upset with me for some reason or other.

At one stage I made plans to move back to Australia while Xanana was still in prison. The decision to leave Jakarta was extremely difficult for me and one that I debated long and hard with him. I felt like I was abandoning him by going back to Australia, but we both came to the conclusion that I was probably getting close to the point where I couldn't sustain the façade any longer and that sooner or later I was going to get caught out. As it turned out, it couldn't have been a better time for me to leave. My time really was up.

So after much discussion, I organised to move back to Australia in late 1995. I planned to fly out on the 5th of January and to start my job in Melbourne as program officer with Australian Volunteers International a week later. Unwittingly, I'd made one of the smartest decisions of my life. In the weeks leading up to my departure I came the closest I had ever been to being caught.

I was aware of the danger I was putting myself in the whole time I was working for the Resistance in Jakarta.

But I think because I was aware of the danger, it just strengthened my resolve to do it, and do it well. I was constantly aware that my phone was probably being tapped and I was always anxious that the Intelligence was watching me. I would get phone calls from Timorese I didn't know and I wondered whether they were spies, trained to pass on information to see how I responded so they could confirm what I was up to. Being discreet was always crucial. Other foreigners doing similar things had been thrown out of Indonesia because they weren't so good at covering their tracks.

I had a British friend who was teaching English in Bandung, a town just outside of Jakarta. She wasn't quite as discreet as she needed to be and wound up getting herself deported. On the way out, as she attempted to plead her case, she called me a number of times from the immigration office. It was probably the worst thing she could have done because it virtually implicated me in her case and activities. Once I was linked to someone like that, I would be investigated by the Intelligence and it wouldn't take them long to work out what I was doing.

I had other not so prudent friends who would come to Jakarta thinking they could be more or less open with the Indonesian authorities about what they were doing. They would do some really stupid things sometimes, like list my telephone number as a contact for them while they were in Jakarta. There were a number of times where I thought,

'This is my swan song, I'm out of here now.' But I guess a cat has nine lives. In the end I just about used up every last one.

In the months leading up to my departure, I became a little more lax in security than I was previously. I knew I was leaving so I wasn't so careful, and I met a few Timorese strangers at my house, rather than in public places which is what I usually did. It was such a busy time, I was handing over my job to someone else, preparing for a new life and a new job in Australia, and I got a bit lazy.

A week before I was supposed to leave I was at home packing a few extra boxes I'd forgotten to send with the first lot I'd shipped. Most of my personal things were already on a ship back to Melbourne so they would be there by the time I arrived in January. The fact that most of my belongings were already out of the house made it much easier for me to disappear, which eventually I did need to do. It was Boxing Day 1995. I'd planned to try to visit Xanana the next day; it would be my last opportunity to get into the prison before I left because it was Christmas, but I woke up the next morning feeling incredibly ill.

The next morning I had to force myself to get out of bed. I felt so sick. At that stage I had no idea what was wrong with me. I made it to the prison and stood there for an hour, shivering and sweating while I was waiting to be allowed in. The same guard who prevented me from getting into the prison every other time I tried was there. He refused to let me in. I went home and bawled my eyes out. I was so sick and I'd missed out on my last chance to see Xanana. It turned out that I had dengue fever.

When I got home my maid told me three men in uniforms had come to the house asking about me. Thank God I hadn't been there. I knew I had to get out of the house and do it in a hurry. I managed to move to a friend's house quickly, shifting the remainder of my belongings in taxi loads. The fever had well and truly kicked in by this stage and I was so sick I thought I was dying. The blood vessels around my fingernails all burst and then coagulated, so my nails went black.

It was the most horrendous experience. I couldn't go to the doctor, I couldn't risk being seen on the streets. What saved me was an amazing support network of friends that suddenly emerged around me. They looked after me, brought me food and my friend Puto massaged my feet at the end of each day. Xanana kept sending live chickens to the house from the prison, instructing Puto how to make chicken stew for me over the phone. It was quite surreal.

I rang my old house and discovered that the Intelligence officers had come back every day and were getting more and more aggressive with my maid, insistent that she tell them something about me.

I felt so guilty for putting her in that situation because she had been so wonderful and faithful. I always made sure that I never told her anything about what I was involved in, precisely for this reason. If she was ever to be questioned she would be telling the truth when she said she knew nothing. It was now early 1996, and the Intelligence obviously had enough information on me and my activities that they would have made my life rather unpleasant before throwing me out.

I knew I had to get out of the country fast, but there was no way I could fly out of the international terminal in Jakarta where my flight was booked. I knew they would be waiting for me at the airport. My neighbours had been questioned and they knew exactly what date I was leaving the country. Fortunately, there were flights from Ambon to Darwin so I flew domestic to Ambon, overnighted there and then flew to Darwin the next day. By the time I flew into Darwin I had completely recovered from the dengue fever. I was so relieved to arrive safely.

A week or so after I arrived, I discovered that the girl who took over my old job in Jakarta had been visited by the Intelligence. They questioned her about me and told her that I was on the black list and I shouldn't ever come back to Indonesia. That was the biggest blow I could ever receive. Xanana was still in Indonesia and I had just taken on a job that required me to travel there four times a year. I felt so guilty, my employers had brought me home to do this job and now I couldn't do it properly. They knew about my involvement in East Timor but they had no idea just how involved I really was.

I was struggling with reintegrating into a normal, middle-class life in Australia after the extremes I'd experienced in Indonesia. Xanana would call me constantly from the prison; once he called me five times while I was out to dinner with friends. He'd call me in the middle of the night or at the end of a 12-hour day when I would be exhausted and want to talk for ages. It was so hard to find my place in Australia again when I was still very connected to Xanana and my old life in Jakarta. I was trying to settle into a new world but I couldn't leave the old one behind. I didn't want to leave it behind completely, I just had to put it to one side so I could move on.

Xanana was finally released into house arrest in February 1999. I resigned from my job with Australian Volunteers International and moved to Jakarta in early March of the same year to set up a small support office for Xanana along with two friends from Portugal. We performed a variety of tasks, administrative and political, to support Xanana in the work he was doing to broker a peaceful solution to the East Timor problem. Obviously Xanana was relieved to be free and we were happy to finally be together but so much was happening inside East Timor and things were moving quickly.

It was a very difficult time. Indonesian President Habibie announced that 'If in a process of consultation' the majority of East Timorese rejected autonomy in favour of independence, Indonesia would grant independence. There was so much uncertainty. We had no idea what the outcome of the whole consultation was going to be, whether the referendum was actually going to take place. There was a lot of militia violence going on to try to derail the process.

The United Nations' involvement was closely negotiated with Xanana and foreign governments were all wanting to keep in regular contact with him to find out what was going on and what he was thinking. The international community could see that he was the key player so they all wanted his interpretation of every possible event that occurred.

We worked until four o'clock in the morning sometimes, drafting and translating reports and correspondence, so there was very little time for us to actually just be together. On the odd Saturday night I would go over to the house with a bottle of wine and we'd just sit around and talk, forget about East Timor for a while and share a few moments of intimacy, but that was very rare. We were teased by those moments when there was a semblance of normality. This is what normal life would be like — something as simple as making a cup of tea in the kitchen or cooking dinner at home together. Xanana was still technically under house arrest so there were guards hanging around constantly and our every move was monitored. The demands on him were really great and I just had to put up with that and do my best to be a support.

When Xanana was finally released from house arrest on 7 September 1999, East Timor was literally on fire. The militia groups were intent on destroying East Timor as payback to the people for voting for independence and they fulfilled their objective. A huge amount of East Timor was destroyed and burnt to the ground. It was extremely disturbing for us to witness and there was the emotional distress of losing friends. The phones in our Jakarta office rang constantly. Friends would call crying, desperate and pleading for help as they fled into the mountains from Dili, while their houses were burning down.

So much has happened since that terrible time after the referendum in 1999. I gave birth to our first child, Alexandre, in July 2000. Two months later Xanana and I were married, and Xanana became the first democratically elected president of East Timor in 2002. Even my old friend Joao, who was released from gaol around the same time as Xanana, is part of the new East Timorese Government, in the foreign ministry. I found it quite difficult when we first came to East Timor after the referendum. The lack of privacy and time available to 'us' was something I had to get used to.

From the time I first knew of Xanana to when I came to know him personally, I've been surrounded by people who idolise him and love him as their leader and for what he symbolises. Most of his time has been spent fulfilling his role as a leader, and now as president. It's nothing new for me to deal with, but now that we have a family it affects us in a different way. It just makes things more difficult, in terms of building a relatively normal family life and a functioning relationship.

It has meant that we savour the time that we do have together all the more and the emphasis is on quality rather than quantity. I still have times where the tension builds up and I come to really resent the imposition on his time and I feel like screaming and putting my foot down. But I've come to be more tolerant. I think I've reached a state of acceptance about it now. I've come to accept the fact that this is a direct consequence of who Xanana is and there's not very much I can do about it.

Having a child has been one of the most joyful things of my life. I didn't expect that I would react to motherhood in the way I have. The pregnancy was unplanned and I was concerned about the timing because of everything that was going on. I was worried about how Xanana would cope with the responsibility of a child on top of all the other responsibilities he had to deal with. It's actually been wonderful for him to have Alexandre. With Alexandre he can just be Daddy and play with him and enjoy experiencing his growth — those simple, primal things you experience as a parent. It's a great relief from his political life where he is always having to perform.

Becoming a mother has helped me to be accepted by the Timorese community. I was worried about how they would receive me because I am a foreigner, that perhaps they would resent the fact that Xanana married outside of his culture. But being a mother has seemed to reinforce my common humanity. There's an immediate bond that is created with other mothers when you go somewhere with a child on your hip.

It has also opened my eyes to a whole new set of issues for women in Timorese society. Things like childcare, reproductive rights, birth control, maternal and child health. So many elements of traditional Timorese society work against women. It's really important that those issues become part of public debate here, as a way of gaining better recognition for women and their role in society. I hope I can use my influence to help begin the mammoth task of changing that.

In June 2000 I established the Xanana Gusmao Reading Room. It is a public space aimed at promoting a love of reading and of fostering pride in the fighting spirit of the East Timorese people. My second 'project' was the establishment of the Alola Foundation in March 2001, a women's organisation which intends to draw local and international attention to the problem of violence against women. I'm aware of the authority and influence I have just through association with someone like Xanana, and I really want to use it to full advantage because there is so much to be achieved here.

At the same time, I do feel a bit overwhelmed and daunted by the prospect of having to fulfil this very public role of First Lady. I've been very much in the background of Xanana's life to date. Obviously, there is nothing that prepares you for the role of First Lady, you can't just go out and do a course on it.

I know there are certain activities and behaviour that are deemed appropriate for a first lady, and then there are those that are not, but I don't pay much attention to that. For me, it's about using my influence to benefit the issues and causes. I hope that being a first lady is not incompatible with that work because it is important to me.

Obviously, I have to be mindful of the fact that Xanana is the one who has been elected by the people, not me. I'm suddenly in a position of influence merely by virtue of being associated with him and some people are bound to see that role as being an abuse of that situation, depending on whether they do or don't like what I'm saying. It would be very easy for Xanana's detractors to use things that I may do or say to attack him politically. I don't want that to happen, but equally I don't want to have to curtail my beliefs and my commitments. I don't particularly embrace the prestige or the power. In many ways I would prefer to have a very simple, ordinary life and contribute in whatever way that I can.

All those years I was working for the Resistance and Xanana was in gaol it never figured in my fantasies that one day I would be sitting here and not only would East Timor be free but I would be married to the president. It's an amazing turn that my life has taken but it was never part of the dream for me.

lee tulloch

lee tulloch

After holding various posts in the magazine world, including a stint in the editor's chair of the first Australian edition of *Harper's Bazaar*, writer Lee Tulloch headed for New York.

For more than 15 years Melbourne-born Tulloch lived abroad, where she penned her first three novels, *Fabulous Nobodies*, *Wraith* and *Two Shanes*. From her New York loft, Tulloch also kept Australian audiences entertained with her sharp social commentary in regular columns for the *Sydney Morning Herald*, *Vogue*, *Elle*, *The Age*, the *Melbourne Weekly* and the *Australian Women's Weekly*.

After the terrorist attacks of September 11 all but destroyed Tulloch's Manhattan neighbourhood, she moved back to Sydney in 2001 where she now lives with her husband and teenage daughter.

You miss certain things when you don't live in the country of your birth. Certain smells, certain sounds and jokes. What I missed most about Australia was the sense of humour. We are so much more irreverent than the Americans. The occasional good laugh with another Australian is something you need deeply when you live in New York. I tried very actively to come back once or twice a year so I didn't feel cut off from Australia because one thing I really loathe is that idea of an expatriate. The whole time I was living in New York people called me an expatriate, but I never felt ex. It suggests you've turned your back on your country or left it behind because you actively dislike it.

Up until last year my husband Tony and I had lived away from Australia since 1985, though we did come back for short periods a couple of times in between. We've moved around quite a lot — four years in New York, four in Melbourne, two years in Paris, then back to New York for another six — but we never considered any country to be the final destination. It was always very important for me to stay in touch with my friends here and to keep up with what was happening. I was always very interested in the way Australians were thinking as well, because I was still writing social commentary in my columns from New York for Australian newspapers and magazines. Losing that connection is a terrible mistake writers who move overseas make. You read a lot of things that make you cringe because their interpretation of Australia is either old or just out of touch. I was determined not to make the same mistake.

All the time I was living in New York I felt very strongly that I was still Australian and still a resident of Australia, but I would not have left if September 11 hadn't happened. We lived five blocks away from the Twin Towers. The neighbourhood we lived in — the neighbourhood I really loved — was destroyed and I didn't have the heart to go and live anywhere else in New York. I felt psychically disturbed, sitting there in my TriBeCa loft, looking over at the huge crematorium that used to be the Twin Towers. I knew I had the discipline to ultimately get over it, but at the time I didn't have the heart to want to try.

I had so many messages from Australian friends saying, 'Come back, come back.' There was such a huge outpouring of sorrow and grief that I thought to myself, 'What am I doing here? I've got all these wonderful, compassionate friends in Australia. This might be the time to go back.'

I feel very good about my decision. I think Australia is at a very interesting point of its development. There is some ugliness and some distressing meanness of spirit — look at the government's treatment of asylum seekers, amongst other things — but I think 50 per cent of the Australian population has become more confident of its place in the world. It used to be that whenever you came back to Australia after living overseas, people would say, 'Oh, what's wrong with you? Didn't it work out for you there?' And then when you left again it was, 'Oh, you're leaving. Aren't we good enough?' You can hear the voices. I think that kind of attitude comes from a lack of certainty Australians have about themselves. But I think people have become more confident, they're much more aware of what they've got now. Even compared to a city like New York that has so much culture and so much happening, and a wonderful mix of people that's like nowhere else in the world. You can't repeat that in Sydney or Melbourne, but why would you want to when Australia has its own great things to offer?

After the Sydney Olympics, in particular, I noticed people here had suddenly decided, 'To hell with it, we're a beach culture. We're not some kind of pseudo-European or English culture. We're Australian and we're going to wear thongs and board shorts to a trendy East Sydney café if we want to. We're going to keep the old station wagon with the beach towels in the back, and the banana lounge in the backyard. If you don't like it, bad luck.' There has been a very definite change since the 1980s when I was living here. Back then, Sydney, in particular, was always trying to be something else.

Most city people are happy to embrace their Australianness, but then again there are still some who don't. Like the people behind some of the housing developments I've seen since I've been back. They make me laugh. There is one in Melbourne, a block of loft-style apartments right in the city called the TriBeCa after the one in New York. Why on earth would you want to live in a super expensive loft in the middle of the CBD just because it's called the TriBeCa, when you can live in a place like Melbourne which is full of incredible gardens and wonderful places outside the city? It used to be that we copied English things, but it seems we are copying New York things now.

Moving around as a family has been difficult, but adversity keeps you together. I think a lot of the problems that crop up in long-term marriages and relationships come out of that sense of familiarity and sameness you get from being with someone for so long. But when you change the scenario by moving around, you kind of have to reinvent yourself, and your relationship to a certain extent. Getting started in a new place also means you need each other a lot more. It can cause tremendous stress but you have to make sure you're not snapping at each other and thinking there's something wrong with your marriage, when it's just the moment causing problems.

Tony and I are both adventurous — foolishly adventurous sometimes. But I think that's the key. When we moved away we weren't chasing money and success, nothing material like that. It was more the experience of living in different cultures that motivated us. You can't put a price on experience. Living amongst different cultures makes you learn a lot about yourself and other people as well. You get a chance to experience how other people think.

You learn a lot when you live in a country where you don't speak the language, like when we lived in Paris. It's an especially important lesson to learn as an Australian. You realise what it's like for all the new migrants who come here — how difficult it is, and how stupid and awkward you feel every day. People just wipe you away as insignificant and it's awful for your ego.

It's interesting to observe the way people of different nationalities relate to things. A New Yorker will relate to a problem in a certain way, which is usually completely different to the way an Australian would handle the situation. Of course the laid-back attitude Australians are famous for is definitely worth celebrating. It's a great way to be but on the flip side it can turn into complacency and smugness. Australians have a tendency to approach a problem with a 'Let's just wait and see' attitude, which is fine, but there are times when you do have to act immediately, which is a much more American way of dealing with things.

The way Americans reacted to September 11 illustrates that point. The feeling immediately was very much, 'Okay, this is a problem and we'd better solve it now. Quickly.' I think I got swept up in that for a moment as well. I remember thinking, 'I've just weighed it up and we'd better move fast. I'm out of here.' That was my New York side talking. It's interesting how you develop certain traits that are characteristic of the culture you're living in. It either happens by osmosis or it's a conscious decision you have to make to survive, especially in a place like New York.

After living there for all those years I realise now that I am more American in some ways, but essentially I am still very much Australian. That laid-back nature is still a part of me, and strangely, it worked very well for me in New York. Even though it's a city full of people thriving on being hyper and neurotic. When things didn't work out the way I wanted I'd say, 'Oh, well. That's fine,' and people would just look at me. 'Oh, that's wonderful. How could you be so zen-like?' Forget zen — I was just being Australian.

The first time I went to New York was in the early 1980s when I was the editor of the first Australian edition of *Harper's Bazaar*. I'd just got the job and was sent overseas to cover the fashion shows and meet the editors of all the other editions of the magazine around the world. I went to New York for a few days and the publisher had booked me into an absolutely huge suite at the Plaza Hotel. I remember taking a bath and looking out onto the city through these big windows, marvelling at the glittering skyscrapers dotted across the skyline.

When I was a kid I loved all those old Hollywood movies from the 1930s set in New York. I used to come home from school at lunchtime if there was an old movie on, I loved them so much. And there I was all those years later, sitting in a bath at the Plaza Hotel and the view through my window was like a scene straight out of a Fred and Ginger movie. I remember thinking, 'God, it's still like that.' All those images I'd seen in the movies actually existed. That old part of New York was still there. I was instantly captivated.

Then of course, what happened next was the mystical thing that happens to everyone who goes to New York. You become enthralled by the incredible energy on the streets. It's almost impossible to quantify or even qualify. I still feel it even now. As soon as I get off the plane at Kennedy Airport — that horrible, ugly airport — my spirits are suddenly lifted. I could go away on a holiday, to Costa Rica,

Melbourne, Paris, wherever, but I'd always be wanting to get back to New York because I missed that intangible energy.

We never planned to settle in New York when we first left Australia. We were actually on our way to Italy. We went to Tahiti first for a month and then on to Los Angeles for another month, which sold me on never, ever wanting to live there. It's so full of freeways, no one walks anywhere, and if you do you're considered suspicious by the police. I could never live in a city where I couldn't walk around. It was a vile experience. Next was what was supposed to be a two-week stop in New York before we finally got to Italy. Well, we never made it to Italy. Once we got to New York that was it.

Tony got a job immediately as an assistant on a *Vogue* shoot, and we both realised that New York was the kind of place where anything was possible. It was so easy to break in there. People were very open, very accepting and willing to give you a break. It's still very much like that, they'll at least listen to you or take a look at what you've got. Frankly, they are that way because they don't want to miss out on the latest thing. They've always got their doors open in case you've got a good idea they can make money out of. I don't mean to make it sound calculating, there is actually a generosity of spirit involved, but it is driven by the need to discover the next big thing.

Being different helps. And if you have a degree of charm and good manners, which I think a lot of Australians do —

educated Australians, anyway — they take you to their bosom instantly. There's absolutely no problem meeting people, which makes getting through those difficult first steps of settling into a new place much easier.

But that's how New York has always been. Generations and generations of migrants have gone there to start a new life. And of course, scores of young artists have gone there in search of inspiration. Sadly, though, I don't think New York is that great a place for young artists any more. Although what I said about people being open and accepting is still true, the city has become so expensive that few young artists can physically survive there. A lot of them have been pushed away from the city into places like New Jersey, which, as a consequence, is probably where you'll find some of the more interesting and challenging art in America.

On an international level, some of the best ideas have come out of New York, but I don't think that's so true any more. Some of the freshest ideas are coming from small towns in places like Ohio, or Adelaide, or Manchester. They're not really coming from the big, famous centres like London or New York now.

New York has become a theme park for very rich people, and the artists and writers who have made it. I think the image of New York as a haven for young, creative talent is a bit tarnished now and it's a shame. But then again, I would never discourage anyone from giving it a go if they can. You can learn a lot from New Yorkers.

New York society is such a meritocracy. It's not just about how much money you have, you are celebrated if you are really good at something. Someone will discover you one day if you hang in there. That guy on the street in the shorts and T-shirt, who looks like everyone else, could be an absolute genius. I met a guy just like that in a café once. He struck up a conversation with me about something obscure, I can't remember exactly what. Later, as I was walking past the newsstand, I saw the same guy on the cover of *Time* magazine.

That's what is so wonderful about New York. It's not about how fabulous your apartment is or whether you can cook that fantastic meal you saw on the television. Oddly enough, people don't care so much about that stuff there. No one cares about the physical things, it's more about the mind and ideas. That's the great lure of a place like New York, perhaps over a place like Sydney, which I think is much less a society of the mind, but more one of physicality, of the body and sensual pleasures.

I grew up watching American television so I thought I was prepared, culturally, to an extent for New York. When you get there, of course, you discover that even the language is totally different. I mean they speak English, but certain Australian expressions, which by the way, you never knew were uniquely Australian, make people's face go blank. Like 'I'm flat out at work'. To that they'll reply, 'Oh, you poor thing. You're lying on the floor, what happened?

Did you break your leg?' Once you've said it you realise it's a colloquial expression, but it takes a long while to unlearn those things. It took me so long to get used to saying things like 'I'm standing in line' instead of 'I'm waiting in the queue'. I think I'm at the point now where those Americanisms will remain in my language forever.

When you drive out of New York into the rest of America, all you see is miles and miles of highway scarred with billboards. And shopping mall after shopping mall. There are pockets of absolutely beautiful countryside and gorgeous houses in the north-east, but essentially American culture is about malls, shopping and getting in your pick-up truck with your backward baseball cap on your head and your shotgun on the back seat. Man after man looks like that. And then in the urban centres there's such incredible ugliness. It's sad because, as a country, they have such great wealth but all they seem to do with it is surround themselves with comfort and fill themselves with lots of tasteless food. The contrast between New York and the rest of America is truly incredible.

I think my wanderlust came from my childhood. Every school holidays we'd head off in the car with the tent and go camping. We used to drive all the way from Victoria to Tewantin, near Noosa, just to visit friends. We'd set off and drive through the back of Bourke and take days to get there, camping in different spots along the countryside and the beaches. We were adventurous. We were a totally happy little family unit.

My parents created a household where anything was possible. If my sister Coral wanted to take drawing classes, she was encouraged. If I said I wanted to be an actress, fine, Mum organised for me to go to drama school. There was nothing in our childhood that had any kind of friction at all. A lot of people think you need to have had a terrible childhood to be a writer, but I don't quite believe it.

I grew up in the suburbs of Melbourne without a whiff of tension, and with totally supportive parents and indulgent grandparents. My primary school was a couple of blocks away from our house and my high school was up the street. Everything I ever needed was in that neighbourhood. My parents still live in that same house. It was blissful and wonderful. Having said that, once I became a teenager I couldn't wait to get out.

I was a bit of an outsider when I was growing up. At the time you think it's horrible, but it's the perfect training ground for a writer because you learn to observe. In my teens I'd go to parties, and while everyone else was getting drunk, I was always the one who had much more fun just watching, waiting to see what everyone would do next. I definitely wouldn't participate. I always sensed what it would be like and I wasn't interested in confirming my suspicions.

I developed a wit really early. Maybe it was all those

movies from the 1930s and screwball comedies I used to watch. Even as a teenager I gravitated towards the work of people like Noel Coward. I guess I just had that kind of sensibility. It's probably why I always got along so well with adults. My daughter's an only child, so of course she's going to be the same because she's never had a sibling. I had my sister but we never got on terribly well as we were growing up. I'd rather be in the kitchen with the adults while they sat around drinking cups of tea, instead of outside playing with the other kids.

I was also very bookish too, my head was always in a book. I started writing very young — at about three years of age. I was a bit of a prodigy, I guess. I'd write funny little verse poems and get them published in the *Sun.* I had written a massive amount of short stories by the time I was 12, most of which I've never showed to anyone. Then, by the time I hit puberty, I was mad about Aussie Rules football. My dad played footy and was very good at it so I guess I picked it up from him. There's a real sense of camaraderie and community amongst footy fans, so I guess it brought me out of my introspective shell a bit.

I wasn't the kind of girl who dreamed about getting married, having kids and living in my own little house in the neighbourhood I grew up in. I think most people aspire to things they never had, and my parents had such a terrific marriage and stable life that by the time I grew up I was about ready for something different. I wasn't quite sure what that was, but I did know that it wasn't a house and three kids in the suburbs. It's interesting because my daughter is almost the opposite, about the suburbs anyway. When we first came back to Australia she was so desperate to live in a house with a white picket fence and a dog in the backyard. She's never actually lived in a house, the entire time we lived overseas we lived in lofts and apartments. Coming back to Australia has meant we can give her that now.

I got involved in the theatre when I was a teenager. Every week I went to the Melbourne Theatre Company's Saturday Morning Club, which was a youth theatre. From the age of 14 I was hanging out with actors. They were incredibly sophisticated, it was wonderful. They were all very arch and witty and fun, so I guess I just emulated them. I'm still quite theatrical.

By the time I was 15, I wanted to be an actress very badly, but I never really had the personality for it. I could never lose my sense of self when I got on stage, which is the most essential thing in acting. I wasn't bad at it, but maybe I would have done better if I'd practised more. Someone wanted to put me in a film when I was about 19 but I said no to the part, I was still at university studying literature. Actors are sort of victims in a way, but I don't mean that in a negative sense. What I mean is that they take other people's words and bring them to life. Obviously they interpret the words in their own individual way, but I'd rather write the words and be making the statement.

My very first job after uni was as a research assistant for the local member for Mordialloc in Victoria. He was a Liberal politician and I was way left. Uni students always are. I wore a black armband when Gough Whitlam was sacked, like everyone else. For some reason though, knowing this, the politician hired me to write his speeches and newspaper columns.

A year later the Liberal Party offered me a job as a research assistant in Canberra. Before I knew it I was working at Parliament House on the Federal backbench committees. I had the ethnic affairs, social welfare, industrial relations and Aboriginal affairs portfolios. It was the most divergent track of my whole career, a total aberration. But you can imagine what I learnt about Australian politics. The other young research assistant working with me at the time was Nick Minchin, who is now a senator and minister in the Federal Liberal Government. Our jobs were a stepping stone to becoming a politician and Nick obviously followed that path, but there was no way I was going to. I knew I wanted to be a writer.

On weekends I tried desperately to write a novel but I just didn't have the discipline. The job was totally fascinating for the first 18 months but towards the end of my final year, I thought, 'What am I doing? I've got to get out of here.' There were so many shenanigans going on behind the scenes that I didn't feel comfortable with the morality of it. People do things to each other in politics just for the hell of it and it was a big boys' club. All these politicians would be sitting in parliament either asleep or guffawing. I used to say that they should televise it, so the public could see what our members really do when they're in parliament. That's not to say I didn't respect some of them. There were politicians I really respected, on both sides of the fence.

Although some of them were there just for their egos. They loved the status their positions gave them. I hated the masculinity of it. As a young, attractive female, I was told by my boss (who hired me) that if there was even a whisper of a rumour of me being involved with any politician, I was fired, whether it was true or not. It was the late 1970s and that was where I, as a woman, stood in the run of things. I was always going to be the scapegoat.

I started looking for another job and found myself in Sydney with a job at *Vogue*. Getting into a magazine in those days wasn't as hard as it is now. *Vogue* advertised the job in the paper (which would rarely happen now, you almost always have to know someone), I applied and that was it. I was the fashion and beauty writer at first, then features editor. At the time, all the girls at *Vogue* were going to a psychic in Manly and I went along once. 'You know, you've got 30 years of this. You're going to be in fashion for 30 years,' she said to me. 'It will take you that long to get out of it.' I'm coming up to my 25th year, so she may have been right.

June McCallum was the editor of *Vogue* when I worked there. She was such a marvellous woman. Not only did she have a visual eye, but having worked in London, she could tell the difference between what was derivative and what was really Australian when it came to fashion.

Fashion is always accused of being trivial but, rightly or wrongly, it has such an impact on how people feel about themselves. Often it is wrongly, but it's still fascinating to observe from a sociological perspective. Fashion isn't just about clothes, it's a powerful way of showing the world what tribe you belong to. Even before I first started in magazines there was quite a lot of intellectual work on the subject by great fashion writers like Kennedy Fraser, who wrote some fantastic pieces for *The New Yorker* in the 1970s.

It was a really great time in Australia then. Australia's identity was starting to come to the fore with the film industry kicking off. All of these great films were coming out and I wrote about the film industry a lot, I even went to Cannes with the Aussies a couple of times. There were all kinds of interesting things happening everywhere. Bands like Mental as Anything were starting to make it big. It was a very fertile time.

After four years at *Vogue* I was restless, so when I was offered another job, at *Woman's Day* in the early 1980s, I took it. Everyone was totally shocked. They couldn't imagine me going to such a down-market publication, but I was really interested in the fact that those magazines had such a mass readership. Many more readers than *Vogue* — 10 times more. But they were talking down to their readers badly, so I took the job with a mission to change that.

I was very naive about magazine politics, but it didn't take me long to realise that the politics I'd witnessed at Parliament House weren't anywhere near as dirty as what went on in magazine publishing, at that time anyway. I was supposed to be jointly editing *Woman's Day* with the man who was the editor in chief, but it didn't work out that way. I felt that the only thing they wanted was a young woman to zap up the image of the magazine and that was about it.

After a year the publishers at Fairfax, who owned the magazine then, said, 'We think you're more talented than this. We want to do a fashion magazine and you've had the experience. What would you like to do?' We decided to launch an Australian edition of *Harper's Bazaar*. It had such a great history in America, even though at that stage it had turned into a bit of a rag in bad need of a revamp.

We didn't have an office for the first few months of the magazine, we worked out of a hotel room. Fairfax had never done a fashion magazine before, so they had no idea about the budgets involved. I had a very tiny team but they were all hyped up and really believed in the magazine. We all worked till midnight most nights.

The creative side of the job was wonderful but it turned out to be a very unhappy experience. The magazine I produced was not what Fairfax was expecting. We did things like put Boy George on the cover, which the publishers could not get their heads around. There was also a lot of pressure to fill the editorial pages with advertisers. Nine issues in I was fired, and given two hours to leave the building. I remember thinking, 'Oh, my God. You work till midnight and you don't have a family life. You live and breathe this thing. You care about it much more than the executives of the company ever do, and then they literally march you out the door.'

I was 30 years old and I'd also got married that year. I'd always wanted to write a novel and decided that then was the time to start. I started a novel about fashion, which eventually became *Fabulous Nobodies.* Just after I starting writing we decided to move overseas, and that's when we eventually landed in New York.

When I look back I don't know how we managed to make the move. We didn't have much money and packing up your life like that with no job or house to go to, or even a firm destination, is such a huge step. But we were both ready to take the leap. Tony was really ready, he was young — only about 21 then — so he was at the stage where he wanted to see the world. I think it was one of those classic stories of the 1980s. You know, young artists coming to New York with little more than the clothes on their backs but somehow managing to scrape things together. We were lucky, too. We always had fabulous apartments that were cheap, but still wonderful. Our first place was this huge apartment in the East Village. It was the whole floor of a brownstone, with marble fireplaces. It was like something out of a Polanski movie.

It was right in the middle of all the great nightclubs, one of which was the famous club Palladium. I remember the first night we arrived in New York, we went to visit a friend who took us to the Palladium for the first time. We thought we weren't dressed up enough, in our black T-shirts and black shorts. 'You're perfectly dressed,' our friend said. That was the great thing about New York in the 1980s, you could go out to a nightclub in a pair of shorts or you could swan about dressed like Diane Brill or Marilyn Monroe in incredible evening gowns, bouffant hair, theatrical make-up and 10-inch high heels. It was extremely lavish and decadent. It was wonderful.

I'd spend most days in our apartment working on my novel, banging away on a manual typewriter. The book was originally meant to be about a magazine editor, but once I got to New York I was captivated by the nightclub scene. All of those curious creatures: the girls who went to the clubs every single night and the all-powerful girls who worked on the door. I started to write and this girl's voice came to me. She worked on the door of a nightclub … and that, eventually, was what *Fabulous Nobodies* was about.

After I finished the first 30 pages I sent them to an agent and he sold the novel to a publisher in a matter of weeks. Now that I've written three novels, I realise just how easy writing that first one was. It was ridiculously easy. But it was also good timing. It was the period in publishing when people like Jay McInerney and Brett Easton Ellis were writing gritty novels about young, downtown New York. I was right in the demographic so they just snapped me up.

Publishers wanted books about yuppies. You know, *Bright Lights, Big City*. Greed. Wall Street stockbrokers and lots of cocaine. All those images of New York in the 1980s were indeed true to life. But what's interesting is the 1990s were probably worse. I was reading something Jay McInerney wrote recently, and I feel the same. He said the 1990s were much more excessive and materialistic than the 1980s, with all the dot coms spawning instant millionaires, most of them extremely young.

There was a certain kind of naivety to 1980s excess. It was all about showing off in a juvenile way, which was quite innocent and lovely. I mean, you'd get into nightclubs for free if you were dressed up enough. Everyone would hang outside the clubs looking at everyone else to see what they were wearing. It was silly and they were all a pack of airheads, but there was something quite charming about it.

I wanted to capture some of that charm and sweetness in *Fabulous Nobodies*. That excitement of being young in

New York, going out to clubs and being able to walk down the street in the most ridiculous, over-the-top outfit without anyone giving you a second glance.

I remember I did a story on the famous New York restaurant, Le Cirque, a favourite haunt of New York socialites. It was when Christian Lacroix had done *pouf* skirts, these enormously flouncy, incredibly expensive skirts, and they were extremely popular with the ladies who lunched. These skirts were sending the staff of Le Cirque insane because they took up so much space, three times more than a person would normally occupy. So you would see all of these otherwise incredibly chic, rich ladies sitting there with their skirts literally puffed up around their necks. It was quite hilarious. And of course, you'd have Donald Trump running around with a string of big-haired young blondes. But that's got nothing to do with the 1980s. Donald Trump is still running around with a string of young blondes. They just have smooth, straight hair now.

I loved going to Paris to the Haute Couture shows. It was so excessive. Dresses were worth $30,000 or more. They were often beaded with real jewels and it would take 25 seamstresses a whole month just to sew the hems. You'd sit in those shows and your spirits would be lifted, and you'd think, 'Yes, I do care about a dress. I do care about that Christian Lacroix gown because it's absolutely incredible, and the wizardry and craft that has gone into making it is amazing.' People say, 'Oh, but that's unrealistic and real women can't wear it.' But I think couture exists on a different, more intellectual level.

Fashion isn't always so glamorous. It's always been a lot of hard work and the bottom line of the business is that it's all about moving merchandise. Over the last decade fashion shows have become public spectacles and a circus for journalists. Models have become valuable commodities. They're not just mannequins any more, they're celebrities. And you can't get backstage for all the video cameras.

Suddenly there were so many more press people wanting to report on fashion, grabbing sound bites, and for the first time fashion stories started hitting the front page of broadsheets like the *Sydney Morning Herald*. Average designers were being acclaimed as geniuses but it was all just hyperbole and no substance. I kind of lost interest in it. It became extremely boring really fast.

When you've been a fashion writer as long as I was, you start to see the same things over and over again. When 1970s flares made their first comeback, I thought it was interesting. Second time around, I thought, well, this is a bit boring but I can use my knowledge of the past to say something about it. But third time around, it was like, 'forget it'. You see 21-year-old fashion assistants marvelling over a particular style of shoe that I've seen maybe 10 times over the years, and yet they think it never existed before.

There are so few elder statesmen in fashion now, it's such a young person's game. The older ones get bumped off to make room for the girls in their twenties, who actually wear and look good in all of that stuff.

In the end I never found writing about fashion and the people in the business particularly satisfying. I got much more out of writing about artists or film or theatre. The tendency for a writer covering fashion now is to send it up, and it's so easy to satirise. It's self-satirising sometimes. But I did that with *Fabulous Nobodies* and I feel no need to repeat it. I think there is far too much of that kind of thing now, so many books and columns full of people writing funny things about fashion.

Obviously, there is also an incredibly dark side to fashion. Inside the business there's a lot of people using other people, and there's a lot of tragedy. The model situation has always been really grim: taking 14-year-old girls and spoiling them, then letting them loose without any real support. Really, it's eating up women and spitting them out. There's a lot of that going on. You have to be a very strong person not to be affected by it, but too often the girls very much are. That's the reason I wrote *Wraith*, to give people a window into that world. The people involved deny it all the time. They'll say, 'Oh, that's not what it's like,' but they damn well know it is.

Most model agents claim their younger models are always chaperoned. 'We put them in a house and we look after them. There's no drugs,' they say. Well, maybe some do, but most of them don't. Thankfully Australian model agencies aren't as bad. Of course, it's not all like that, there are some terrific people in the business who do care.

I've met a million young models who go to Paris or Milan. Their agents put them up in a share apartment with five other models and they spend their days traipsing around town with their portfolios on 'go sees'. Which is fine, but you have to remember that these girls are often still children, and they're thrust into this world of adults, most of them strangers. One girl told me about a fashion photographer her agency sent her to see. He opened the door with a full erection and a shoe hanging off the end of it.

Most people in the business aren't seriously psychopathic, but many of them are so self-absorbed that they are very careless about how they act in front of 14- and 16-year-old girls. So they'll take drugs in their presence without even registering the thought that it may not be appropriate. You meet agents who find no fault with encouraging girls to smoke, because, after all, it keeps them thin. And if she's thin, she'll get more work and everybody makes more money. That's when she stops being a girl and becomes a product, something to sell. That's just how the business works.

Unfortunately, however, all the bad press doesn't stop young girls sending their photos into model agencies in droves. Models have replaced movie stars and so many young girls dream of being a supermodel. These days, everyone wants to be famous quickly without having to work hard at it or pay their dues. And their parents encourage them, spurred on by dreams of their 15 year old making the family an extra $100,000 or $200,000 a year.

There's a lot of ego involved on the girls' part too. These young girls, often from small towns and poor countries, are sent to big, fast cities like Paris or New York and most of them have never been away from home before. They get invited to glamorous parties, they get into nightclubs for free and because then they attract swarms of men, often they eat and drink for free, too. New York is full of guys who will only date models.

The issue of body image is probably the most dangerous, and it will continue to be for as long as clothes are supposedly meant to look best on extremely skinny teenage girls. There's no doubt some of them do look incredibly gorgeous in pictures, and I admit I'm still capable of being captivated by those images and disassociating myself from the fact that there's a big chance the girl's a chain-smoking monster who lives on laxatives. The beauty of the photographic image makes you forget about all of that, momentarily.

When we lived in Paris I met a lot of young models from eastern Europe. There was one girl Tony photographed. She was absolutely beautiful, she should have been one of the world's top models. She was so desperate to make it because she would have been the shame of her family if she failed, as she had to send the money she earned back home to help support them. She was naturally thin but she tried to diet herself even thinner, thinking she'd get more work. Tony photographed her a few times and by the last sitting she had got to the point where fine hairs had developed all over her body, which is often what happens with anorexics. It's very hard to get to the top of that industry. The money involved in the top ranks is ridiculous. We're talking millions. I guess some girls believe it's worth starving themselves for. It's really sad because there are so many girls like that one in Paris who don't quite make it, as gorgeous as they are.

You'd think being surrounded by beautiful young girls would give any woman over the age of 30 a complex, but for some reason it never gave me one. I think worrying about your age is ridiculous. There's nothing you can do about it so why not be proud instead? I still cannot fathom why people want to hide their age. It should be a badge of honour.

These days, turning 40 is nothing. When I turned 30 it was supposed to be a big drama, but it didn't bother me, neither did turning 40. I have so many fantastic friends in their fifties who look as if they have at least another 50 years to go. You get to the point where you realise that your age is just a number. And I've never been good at maths anyway.

libbi gorr

libbi gorr

Satirist, writer and presenter Libbi Gorr first burst onto the airwaves in the late 1980s as part of the team on 'Kick to Kick' — the popular AFL comedy program on Melbourne radio station 3XY. It was there that Gorr's bold alter ego, Elle McFeast, was born.

Gorr's slicing wit made Elle — part Aussie Rules groupie, part brassy broad — one of the best-loved characters of the 1990s. But it wasn't all just bawdy humour. McFeast's womanly curves and wanton, albeit exaggerated sexuality was an affront to popular images of beauty and femininity. She quickly became a poster girl for the revolt against the stick insect stereotypes which dominated the media and pop culture.

In 1991 Elle McFeast made her television debut on ABC TV's 'Live and Sweaty'. In 1994 the first of many McFeast specials hit the small screen including 'Sex, Guys and Videotape', which won a gold medal at the New York Festival of Television.

'McFeast Live' hit ABC TV in 1998 but the controversial Chopper Read incident threw an unexpected fork in Gorr's road. Last year's documentaries 'Sex Cells' and 'The Queen and I' became the last of the McFeast specials and the birth of a new era.

After more than a decade, McFeast was put to rest and her creator introduced the world to a sassy new personality to be reckoned with — Libbi Gorr.

I grew up in a very loving, rough-and-tumble kind of home with two beautiful brothers — David, who is three years older than me and Jon, who's three years older than him, so I was the youngest and the only girl. My parents are both devoted to their family and would still do anything for us, anything except provide traditional, stereotypic role models, that is!

I was thrown into an all-girls school from the very early age of five, so I was surrounded by gracious women dedicated to curbing stomping on stairs and taming recalcitrant ponytails. My mother worked full-time as a pharmacist and my father ran a car workshop in

Murrumbeena, Victoria — the quaintly suburban nook of Glen Eira that spawned Daryl Braithwaite, Arthur Boyd, Melbourne football hero Robbie Flower and the legendary maker of Bob Downe, Mark Trevorrow. I like to think of Murrumbeena as the Cuba of Caulfield. It has its own identity.

Every day Dad would pick me up from my posh private girls' school and I'd spend the rest of the afternoon with him, answering the phones amongst the grease and oil and petrol. Here my playmates were big blokes with names like Black Max and Wing Nut and Parrot.

It was such a contrast to my ladies' college life: hat and gloves, 'Don't eat on the street, girls, up and down on the left-hand side of the stairs, girls.' Dad made sure, however, I could ride along on his Harley, sidesaddle.

Achievement was very important in my childhood. There was never any question that my parents' expectations of me were any different to what they expected of my brothers just because I was a girl, so it seemed like anything was possible. I've never seen my gender as anything apart from a sometimes delicious and sometimes perplexing point of difference.

You see, throughout my childhood, both at home and at school, I got a very strong message that men and women were the same. But I think the message somehow got confused. Yes, women should have equal opportunity, equal rights and equal pay, and there shouldn't be any gender divide when it comes to a person's value to society. But that doesn't mean we're somehow the same.

There will always be fundamental differences between men and women in how they deal with things and perceive the world. I think you learn more and more about those differences as you get older. Obviously there are some elements of human nature that are universal and carry through the genders — such as the capacity for feelings and emotions, and the desire to be loved, and the desire for comfort. And the desire for chocolate. Oh yes. Don't think a sweet tooth is the domain of the sisterhood.

After I finished high school I decided to study law. I was still at uni when I started work experience with Tim Lane, the celebrated cricket commentator and football guru in the 3LO Sports Department. It was a great place to learn: the boys at 3LO would let me do strange little things like cover the Pan Pacific School Games.

I kept on doing little bits and pieces like that while I was at uni so I had something to live off, coupled with oh-to-be-forgotten stints as a waitress where cooks would lock me in the fridge for fun. When I finished law I was accepted for my articles, which is your professional year, but I put it off for three years while I ran around in flouncy skirts and tight corsets singing cheeky, bawdy songs in pubs with a cabaret act called The Hot Bagels. The Bagels was the first avant-garde kink in my road.

The Hot Bagels was a highly emotional, volatile, all-girl group and I was the last to join the final incarnation. I ran around the world with The Bagels for a few months. I even tried stand-up for the first time in London but I failed dismally, so I ended up back in Melbourne on the wireless, this time as Elle McFeast.

Her story is a beauty. It was late 1988 and I borrowed a tape recorder from Tim Lane and went to 3XY where there was a football show called 'Kick to Kick', hosted by Peter 'Grubby' Stubbs. They used to do send-ups, interviews and comedy sports — the kind of thing Melbourne is famous for. There were no girls on the team so I just turned up one day and pleaded, 'Can I do funny interviews with footballers for you?' They thought I looked good with a microphone so they gave me a go and offered to pay me $20 every second week, if they had it.

You had to be grateful for a little bit of on-air space in those days. But Peter Stubbs was extraordinarily generous and supportive. Trevor Marmalade also worked on the show and he and I soon developed a brother/sister-type relationship. It was an innocent kind of sibling rivalry. But he was very good, even then — so prepared, so smart, so clever and savvy.

I'm eternally grateful for that starting point, but I also helped it happen. Radio is fiercely competitive and I had to pester to get in. It wasn't a gender thing. It's radio. It was more like, 'Can I play? Can I play? Can I play?' and finally they gave in. That's just media. Clarke Hanson, another generous man and my original contact point in the 3LO Sports Department, told me that.

I wouldn't be where I am if a lot of very generous men, who weren't threatened by my enthusiasm, had not helped me along the way. There was never anything more to it other than mentoring, never any sexual patronage (dammit ... cos some of those guys were pretty all right). I think they were just pleased to find someone so excited and enthusiastic about the things they also loved.

After putting it off for two years, I finally decided to do my articles while I was still working on 'Kick to Kick'. The law institute let me continue doing interviews at lunchtime, mostly because the lawyers loved meeting the footballers. They would throw partners' lunches and invite Simon Madden and Dermott Brereton. I had a fabulous time, and considered myself great value for money, for not only as an article clerk did I photocopy and do company searches, I'd bring footballing entertainment into the office as well.

It was a bit of a dog-leggy start. But working out what I wanted to do with my life just wasn't clear cut, so it was important for me to have a couple of irons in the fire. Sometimes you have to fulfil commitments in certain areas of your life, which for me was law, before you have the confidence to pursue what you really want.

There are some great women working in sports radio and sports media now: Elaine Canty, Karen Tye and Dixie Marshall, who was my friend when I first started. She was a sports nut. The ABC gave many women their first break in the 1970s.

I remember seeing an ad a few years ago for a part-time female sports reporter. Were they looking for a part-time female, or a part-time sports reporter, I wondered? But getting back to the point, the change in legislation allowed a bunch of chicks to get through the door. I don't think that point can be made strongly enough. Had the government not implemented equal opportunity, those doors may never have been opened. Now there are many women who have had very long, successful careers in sports journalism. Like Caroline Wilson, who is the head football writer at the *Age* in Melbourne. It's really just a choice for women now: do they want to spend their waking hours living in a world of sport?

I'm a child of the 1970s, and we are a particular breed of adventure girl that came through thinking we could have a go at anything. One of my friends says that we are the era of discontent because so much was said of what we could achieve, but no one told us there are boundaries in life.

We believed we could have everything. And not just everything, but fundamentally everything all at once;

emotional happiness, financial stability, career fulfilment. Of course that's not how it turned out. I found myself included on that roller-coaster ride, along with all the other 35 year olds who closely examined their lot when they discovered there were boundaries in life, boundaries to being human. But as Stephen Wright says, 'You can't have everything. Where would you put it?'

I think life skills should be taught to kids early on. Understanding how to deal with life is just as important as being able to add up. Quite frankly, it might do away with the need for all this therapy when you get into your thirties. It's not like life is straightforward, there are lots of adventures and wonderful things that can happen. But you will also make mistakes along the way and it would save us all a lot of heartache if we knew not only how to deal with them a little better, but that making them is all part of living.

Oh God, what a relief that is! To be grateful for the mistake! You ask me about 'McFeast Live' and the Chopper Read interview? Everyone asks me about that, and although I'd prefer they'd at least introduce themselves first, I can understand why.

As volatile as the situation looked on the outside, it was more within myself. Chopper wandered onto the set shickered and I — so prepared and so focused on making a success of the very first show of a long-awaited new series — continued the interview asking questions about how much of his work was fact and how much fiction. To illustrate, he read excerpts from his best-selling books and, well, the place was in uproar. It went beyond television. But you see I'm a risk taker — always have been, and always, to some extent, will be. And that can have consequences, some great and some not so great.

Certainly from the fallout one would think I had had the career in toe cutting, not Chopper! But at the end of the day Eric Bana didn't play me in the movie. That's something I'm gonna have to sort out for myself. Flicking through one of those lovely spiritual books you get in candle shops I found a wonderful saying: 'One learns more from their mistakes than their successes', and I have to say that in the matter of McFeast and Chopper versus all, that's very true. Certainly, I'd never attempt an interview with a notorious, drunken, literary crook without wearing a bra ever again.

They were black days but it was a wonderful lesson and an extraordinarily important learning curve. It taught me about the karmic nature of TV, it taught me about keeping my mouth shut. It taught me that not everything's about me. That was a nasty shock. It taught me that I can get to a size 10 if I'm upset enough. It taught me it's no fun being a size 10 if you feel like shit. It taught me about all sorts of things. Mostly about people and consequences.

The whole experience was actually an epiphany. It was a very important and positive event. We went on to make more specials; one called 'Women In Uniform' was selected for an international film festival in Texas. The ABC threw in a small amount of development money to do a pilot for a low-budget international series while we were there promoting the film, but then management eruptions at the ABC meant the editing facilities were cancelled before we even got back to Australia. So I set up a production company with former boss of the ABC, David Hill, called Gorr Hill — that made us laugh. To cut a long story short, that's how my new life began. 'The Queen and I' and 'Sex Cells' ended up on TEN. Both have recently been bought by Oprah's TV station Oxygen in America (I just needed to share that with the group). And I didn't need a few good men to win my own personal battle with myself about my future. I only needed two. David Hill and producer/director Stewart Burchmore. We walked three abreast the whole way. Though mine were infinitely the nicest, I reckon.

Possibilities do come out of total breakdown, it's true. Success is the best revenge. Hell hath no fury. Don't get mad, get effective … all of that. But once that was done, once the chip was off the shoulder and back in the chocolate ice cream where it belonged, it made me stop and re-evaluate, and work out why I was doing this. What on earth was driving me? I realised it had nothing to do with Elle. It was about me, Libbi.

I'm not the first person who has used a character to be brave, to do things that maybe I was too afraid to do as myself. There are plenty. Barry Humphries has a very problematic relationship with Dame Edna, even though Dame Edna is much more of a caricature than Elle became. Maybe I didn't have a very strong identity or sense of self because everything I had achieved was based on me being Elle.

It's just very hard to have proper human relationships with people when you are in character 24/7. I've met lots of people but I never got to speak to them as myself. You can't make friends as a character, you can't allow anyone to penetrate it because then it loses all of its power. If we were meeting each other and I was Elle McFeast, you'd exist for me, for my career. You wouldn't feel like you knew me any better than the minute we first met and you'd think that I had an agenda in meeting you. I still find it weird that people would think Elle McFeast was my real name.

Being Elle took up so much time that there was little left for a real life. TV is a pretty hungry beast and you have to keep feeding it to keep it alive. And that's exactly what we did for seven years, with a month off here and there. But it was always exciting and at that stage I didn't really care about what it might eventually do to me. I didn't care about those things in my twenties.

Life away from McFeast is just as exciting, if slightly less manic and all consuming for the time being. I think the proper word is 'balanced'. That's the one they use in Special K ads. Balanced. Healthy on the inside.

It does take a while to work out what gets you out of bed in the morning, and those things do change as you move through the journey of life. In your twenties it's the excitement of winning and getting there. But once you've been around a little longer things happen that show you there's more to life than the race. Life is not necessarily all about winning but about stopping along the way to help someone or to take a look at the view. It's actually a journey and it's important to make it as enriching as possible. It's the whole 'tortoise and hare' thing. You have to work out how many eggs are in which baskets.

Being impulsive is great in one respect, but you really do need to think things through sometimes. But then again, you can't think about things too much or else no one would ever start anything. You see, philosophy is everything. It's the therapy of the new millennium. And no, I still don't have a definite answer. It's all to do with my inner Libra.

I think it's better to see your life as a surf in the ocean rather than a roller-coaster ride. A roller coaster has ups and downs, and if you have extraordinarily high ups you have to expect extraordinarily low downs. But surfing requires a lot more skill. You don't just have to hold on and hope for the best; you're actually in control of what's happening, to an extent anyway. When you're in a tube, you try to stay there and get ready to catch the next one. Or you can have a little sun-bake on your board while you're waiting for the next good bunch of waves to come along. It's about skill, daring and confidence — not just buying a ticket on the ride. Always remember sunscreen though. No one wants to get burnt.

All this has been part of the first chapter of my public life. The lovely thing about having a first chapter is that there's a second one where you can choose different ways to express yourself. It doesn't have to be based on the initial model. I'm happy to wait and see what happens next. My channel is open. I just enjoy having a play.

Friendship has been very important in my life. Real friendships. I've got a remarkably eclectic, delicious group of friends. At least I did at the time of writing! Lovely, great, creative, smart and very tolerant people. All with a slightly larrikin streak. I like friends. They are my hobby. More high maintenance than stamps but oh-so-fulfilling.

I've met some amazing people in my life. I always remember Paula Yates in particular. I met Paula two months before she died. I'd never seen anyone so broken, it makes me too upset to think how broken she was. How full of life and full of love, but her heart was in pieces.

Meeting James Hewitt was an interesting experience. I wanted to meet James because I was interested in seeing why Princess Diana loved him so much. She risked a huge amount to be with that man. Once we met it was obvious why, he was very charming. We were planning to use the interview with James in one of my specials. We got all the footage we needed, but in the end we decided not to use any of it. We had to make a choice: did we want to expose that private part of Princess Diana's life or should we just let everybody be? We chose not to stir that particular pot.

That's an important lesson to learn as well. Which way do you want to go creatively? Do you want to press buttons of hurt, exploit people's insecurities and explore their hurt or do you want to create joy?

The second part of my story was about getting back into the saddle. The third part was realising that I needed more skills so I went back to school to study script writing. That in itself was an experience. Everybody in my class was at a life junction. Everybody. Even the teachers. It was fabulous. It was just like *The Big Chill* except no one died in the first 10 minutes.

There's something to be said for jumping into another pool or doing a U-ey like that. Even summoning the courage to just have a go is difficult. But the bottom line is that you are rewarded for courage. If you are at the point where you can't live another moment in your present circumstances, you have to take the leap. It is scary but if you don't make the jump the new road won't exist anyway. The rest will unfold.

That's what I mean about the journey. I'm really glad I'm having the opportunity to live it because I didn't when I was on TV. In a way I created my own world so I didn't have to relate. I didn't have to use my own courage.

And courage is just like a muscle in the body: if it doesn't get any exercise it won't work properly. That's the truth about many qualities.

There are lots of things in life you cannot control, but the most important thing to understand is that you can't control each other. You only have authority over yourself and your own feelings and the way you react to things. It's not what happens that matters. In the end the only thing that really matters is how you deal with it. Everyone is their own person and there are karmic forces that unfold as they should. And there's a lot to be said for going with the flow. Paul Keating allegedly once said to his cabinet, 'If it looks like you're hammering a square peg into a round hole, then boys — start banging.' I don't necessarily agree with that any more. Which isn't to say Keating's personal appeal has diminished in the least. I still think he's a sex machine.

Life is tough and overwhelming sometimes but the answers to the way out of those difficulties are often inside you. You just have to stop talking and listen a bit. Intuition is something that should be noted, particularly gut feeling — it tells you quite clearly. It's easy to construct elaborate reasons for why things happen and to over-intellectualise, but the truth is, some answers are very simple. You just need the courage to stop hiding behind all the drama you create and recognise that.

The children in your life are the ones that make you realise that you're not the centre of the world. The simple pleasure of curling up, eating potato gems and watching *Chitty Chitty Bang Bang* on a Sunday night with the children in my family are joyous moments that can't be replicated anywhere else. That might sound dicky, but it's true. Ultimately, I think creative people and children speak the same language. It's all about imagination. And potato gems, of course.

But in the end, biologically, we are animals underneath and when you get to 35 and you can feel yourself ovulate, you know someone's trying to tell you something. I would love to have my own children — a lot of my friends who have children say you don't have to be in the perfect situation to have them, and you can't wait for that perfect situation to come because it probably never will. You just have to do it.

I think both you and your partner have to really want children and be ready for them. It's a project — a lifelong project — and one that I hope to partake in somewhere along the line. We just have to work out where everything fits!

After all, it's the simple things that sustain us — like love, relationships and the occasional new frock. Crikey. I could stand up on the back of a boat and start singing the songs from *Yentl* any minute.

liz broderick

liz broderick

In 2001 lawyer Liz Broderick was named Telstra NSW Business Woman of the Year, as well as Telstra Australian Corporate Business Woman of the Year. As a partner in one of Australia's biggest law firms, Broderick has driven change in the legal profession by introducing family-friendly initiatives to the industry.

She also participated in an international study conducted by the Organisation for Economic Co-operation and Development into family-friendly policies for the workplace and was invited to represent the business sector on a steering committee set up by the Federal Government to advise on the OECD study.

She speaks regularly at local and international forums.

I've always been surrounded by women — I come from a family of three daughters. One of my sisters is in fact my identical twin. My parents chose to send us to different schools, even from kindergarten. Every morning my sisters went off to their school and I went to mine — all of us went to all-girls schools. It was amazing. I think Mum and Dad did that because they felt competition between siblings, twins especially, could be very destructive, and I agree.

Because my sister Jane and I are identical twins, we used to have tremendous fun with the fact that sometimes people couldn't tell us apart. We'd go to each other's schools to see if anyone would notice. Once, Jane did my science exam and I went to her German class. I still remember that day. I'd never spoken a word of German in my life but I managed to fool the teacher for the entire lesson, although I didn't fool her best friends who were in on the secret. It just shows how bad her German must have been!

Despite the fact that we went to different schools we were still very alike and mirrored each other in a lot of ways when we were growing up — in our final year at high school we were both school captains. Our whole family was and still is very close. My father was career oriented, he was the first nuclear medicine physician in Australia and my mother, who was a physiotherapist, always worked, so I never dreamed that my sisters and I wouldn't go on to have careers as well.

Dad always involved us in his work. After school and during holidays we'd go to his surgery and run errands which, as we became older, involved us picking patients up from the hospital and driving them to the surgery for treatment. I remember picking up one particular older lady one day. She asked me if I had any brothers. When I said no, she sighed loudly and exclaimed, 'Oh no! Your poor father. He must be so disappointed. He'll have no one to follow in his footsteps.' I was completely astounded — I couldn't believe people still thought like that. Not too many years later my younger sister graduated from university as a sports medicine physician and my twin sister became an academic. Dad was very proud indeed.

The attitude that girls could do anything was constantly reinforced when I was at school in the late 1970s, which was probably why I was so shocked at the old lady's comment. I was always taught that women could be anything they wanted, whether that was a physician, like my sister became, an academic or a lawyer. It was a very empowering environment to grow up in.

It wasn't until I got into the workforce that I encountered people who suggested that women weren't as capable just because of their gender. It was unbelievable to me.

In the mid-1980s, at the beginning of my career, I moved to London to get some experience. I got a job as a lawyer and it wasn't so much that I was a woman that got in my way. Actually, it was more that I was a foreigner and that I wasn't a graduate of Oxford or Cambridge, which I quickly gathered was a useful (albeit unspoken) pre-requisite to becoming a respected part of the British legal establishment. Luckily, I was working in technology law, which was a new area that few people were qualified in at that stage (I was one of the few people who combined a computer science degree with a law degree in those days), so they had nobody else to choose from. It wasn't like they could race out and hire a bloke instead.

Actually, because I wasn't working in a traditional area of law, I didn't encounter much discrimination or chauvinism at all. However, it was still a very masculine culture to slot into and a lot of it excluded women by default really. Like the fact that networking and meeting new clients would often take place at what you would call traditional men's events. Things like the football or the cricket, or over a single malt whisky at a gentlemen's club.

I've worked for some wonderful men over the years who have been great mentors to me. I can't say that I've had a lot of female mentors, particularly during the early years of my career, but I attribute that to the fact that there was a real absence of women at the top in those days.

Interestingly, in the past — say ten years ago — many of the women you did find at the top in the legal profession were more the men-in-skirts-types who believed that the only way to the top was to emulate the men who were already there and to be as tough, if not tougher than them. Which is fine, but once they climbed to the top of the ladder, they seemed to just kick it out from under them. Nurturing the next generation didn't seem to figure on their list of priorities; in fact I have many female lawyer friends who will tell you that the toughest and meanest bosses they've ever had were women, not men.

I know that many of those women had to work harder than their male counterparts to get to those positions, so perhaps they were trying to toughen up the girls to prepare them for what they anticipated would be the same path. Except it wasn't really, not in my experience anyway. I do believe that, in some instances, women still need to work harder than men to be noticed and to prove themselves but I don't think it's quite as aggressive a climb as it was 20 years ago.

The whole world has changed a lot since then and the legal world has moved along with it, to an extent. There are many more women in senior positions in the corporate world now which means that, as lawyers, many of the clients we are dealing with are also women. And because of that, we've developed a networking culture of our own.

I think a lot of professional women believe that having children will hinder their careers, and it certainly can a lot of the time, but it turned out to be the opposite for me. Granted, I had already been made partner in my firm before I became pregnant, and I was 36, so I'd reached a certain level that did make it easier for me to combine a family and career, but I think my career actually took off after I became a mother. Believe it or not, the skills that you learn from being a mother are totally transferable to your career, even in something like law. You become so much more empathetic and you start to view people more as human beings rather than superiors, colleagues, employees and clients, or whatever other category the corporate code determines. And, interestingly, that makes a great difference to the way they react to you and do business with you. Even at the top end of town. I think you also become more organised and focused because you realise that inefficiency at work translates to less time with your family.

Becoming a mother made me acutely aware of the way corporate culture makes it very difficult for a woman to maintain her career trajectory once she has a child. Motherhood and working 100 hours a week to get that promotion or partnership are just not compatible. There's no point in having children if you're never going to be around long enough to actually raise them. That motivated me to do whatever I could to change it and, as a consequence, it opened up a whole new world.

Even before I announced my first pregnancy, which was seven years ago now, the non-family-friendly nature of corporate culture became a real issue for me. But it was on a business level rather than a personal one that I was able to do something about it. One afternoon at work one of my lawyers popped into my office to tell me she was pregnant. The same afternoon another senior manager came to see me with the same news. What they didn't know was that I also was pregnant. Three weeks later a fourth lawyer joined the mother-to-be queue. That was half my entire team, which I just couldn't afford to lose in one go. And I didn't want to lose them, nor did I want my own career to be halted.

And that's the point really. What's holding women back today is not so much direct discrimination, it's just that to get ahead in corporate culture, law especially, your job has to be your number one priority. And of course, anyone who has a family knows that your kids and your partner will always come first — and so they should. So what often happens in large law firms is that when a woman comes back to work after she's had the baby she realises that it is just not possible to keep on working the long hours she used to, certainly not without any flexibility. And usually she decides that she just doesn't want to. More often than not she'll leave and take up a part-time job in a more flexible environment like a community law centre, and often her career hits a plateau while she's busy raising her kids.

I think that women have a much wider view of what they want in life. A highly paid job isn't enough for most women and it shouldn't have to be. They want to have a wonderful relationship with their partner, they want to love and spend time with their children, they want to enjoy their own time. But the way corporate culture is right now makes it extremely difficult to have all of that and a career that stimulates and remunerates them well. So they make a choice. They vote with their feet and leave.

Obviously it happens across the board in all professions the statistics prove that. If you're talking specifically about law, for the last 10 years about 50 per cent of law graduates have been female, so theoretically the number of women attaining partnership should be evening out. Right? Unfortunately not. While there has been a small increase in the number of women attaining partnership, only 15 per cent of partners in Australian law firms are women. But it's hardly surprising really when you consider that in the world of law, the only way to make partner is to work incredibly hard, long hours with unwavering, consuming commitment.

When I first started out in law almost 20 years ago now, all of us — men and women — were prepared to work ourselves to death for the job. We accepted it would take over our lives. But as I got older, I and many of the lawyers I know grew weary and less tolerant of how demanding it was on our lives. These days, you'd be hard-pressed to find many women who are prepared to do that any more, and increasing numbers of men who are starting to reject that backbreaking culture as well. Lawyer and author Richard Beasley summarised it perfectly in the title of his novel about a Sydney lawyer who gives up his career acting for the poor and abused for a job in a swish city law firm with a big salary, an office with views of the harbour and 23.5-hour working days: *Hell Has Harbour Views.*

It has taken some convincing to get many people in my firm to come around to the idea of a flexible working environment, which is the only way to allow women to keep moving forward in their careers after they've had children. It wasn't just about changing a few people's minds, it was about creating a fundamental shift in the culture that has ruled the corporate world for decades — not just in relation to women, but to men as well. I think men are sometimes the silent victims in this too. A lot of executives would rather be at home with their families at 9.00 p.m. on Monday night instead of at the office. The impact on women is more obvious, because, as the primary carers of children, they are usually the first to cave in or simply walk away from that pressure, whereas it's harder for men to take a stand because they are still considered to be the breadwinners in most families, so they accept it as their lot and suffer quietly.

The biggest obstacle in getting the business world to come around to this way of thinking is the perception that 'flexibility' somehow compromises the 'might' of a hard-hitting business, that it somehow amounts to going 'soft' and will diminish the business' profitability.

In reality, the opposite is true. A business actually loses money when it has to keep replacing its highly trained female staff. If you consider the cost of constantly re-hiring — recruitment costs and training costs — a business actually saves money by retaining staff and giving them the choice to work part-time, a reduced working week or from home some of the time. We tried out a few different ways of working before we came up with a system that worked.

We developed a program where the ultimate responsibility for matters rested with the individual, whether or not they worked full- or part-time. And if a flexible worker needed to come in on a non-designated work day and could not arrange childcare at short notice, they could bring in the kids. They also agreed to carry a mobile phone when away from their home, and to access their e-mail account at least once a day. I wanted each of our flexible workers to remain just as committed to the firm as they had been before they had their maternity leave, and this meant that they maintained their previous position and level of seniority.

I'm lucky that I've been able to have a say about these issues as I know a lot of women don't have the opportunity. I think the majority of women don't have much of a voice when it comes to the terms of their employment. Instead, they are presented with a set of rules and conditions, and are given the choice to accept them as they are, or find another job. There is no room for negotiation or flexibility.

Obviously the government needs to be involved but, aside from the paid maternity leave, a family-friendly workplace does not seem to be on the agenda. Even more pressing than this is the issue of childcare becoming tax deductible. Unless you're earning a substantial salary it's almost not worth a woman returning to work, when you consider that it can cost 20–30,000 dollars a year just for childcare. So if you're earning a salary of say 50,000, you end up working five days a week for just 10,000 a year. And if you're earning less it makes it even harder. It's hardly worth the trouble really and it's little wonder that so many women choose to give up work entirely — it just doesn't make economic sense to go back to work full-time.

Sometimes I do feel a little overwhelmed trying to juggle everything in my own life. And having won the Telstra NSW Business Woman of the Year award this year, my public role has increased dramatically — I think I've spoken at 50 different conferences this year already and we're only halfway through. It is difficult for me to find the time in-between my work and trying to be a good mother to my own children. My two are still so young — six and four — so they really need me.

I do feel guilty about the fact that my career sometimes takes away from the time I have with my children. But I think as a working mother you just have to accept that you will always feel a degree of guilt about not being with your children 24 hours a day. You just have to get on with it. Your children will benefit much more from being raised by a woman who is happy and fulfilled and who can bring that passion and fulfilment into her role as a mother.

I feel so passionate about making an impact and helping to transform the workplace for women, so I guess that drives me to keep going. And I do get a real buzz out of it. As I get older, I'm much more focused on channelling my energies into something that has meaning and bringing my personal values into my working life. And I guess that comes from being a mother — I'm so much more aware of the social impact of what I'm doing and the culture I'm a part of. As a business woman, my decisions don't just focus on financial considerations to the exclusion of everything else. Sure, the financials are important but I also think the social and environmental impact of the business is worth considering. At the end of the day the business needs to be sustainable.

I thought long and hard before I decided to have a baby. Back then, I was really worried that my life and my career would grind to a halt if I had a child so I deliberately put it off until I was 34 years old, eight years after my husband and I got married. Funnily enough, when we were finally ready to become parents my body decided (independently of me, it seems) that it was not. I think that's something a lot of women don't realise — the longer you put it off, the more difficult it is to actually become pregnant. Your fertility at age 34 is just not what it was at 26. It took me two years to fall pregnant, with the help of many ovulation kits. (I recommend them to anyone!) That was a tough time for me. My whole life I've been a high achiever and a problem solver and here I was confronted with something I had no control over, that I couldn't just fix. I got to the stage where I wondered if it was ever going to happen. Eventually it did and I'm so grateful for that; being a mother has changed my life.

Most of the women I know have put off having children until their early and mid thirties. Even in my own family — my twin sister was 34 before she had her first child and our younger sister had her first at 33 years of age. You really have to be ready to have a baby because it changes your life like nothing else you can imagine. Not just because of the impact it has on your career, but your day-to-day life will be radically different. There are women who say that their life just carried on as normal when they became mothers, but you do have to make concessions, there's no getting around it. And if you're really ready you'll actually welcome those changes to your life because they are so transformational and wonderful. I had my babies when it was right for me.

Being a mother has taught me some incredible things. I now understand that I can't control everything and I can't always make things better or fix them, and not everything needs to be fixed anyway. That surrendering of control took a little getting used to.

I remember when Tommy, my six year old, had his first day at pre-school. I took the day off from work so I could drop him off and pick him up. I drove past the pre-school at morning tea time just to check on how he was going and he was sitting all alone, separate from the other kids who were huddled in a big group. I drove past at lunchtime and again he was sitting alone while all of the other kids clung together.

I was heartbroken for him and felt this overwhelming need to make the other kids welcome him into their group. I panicked and called my husband, Hunter, at work. 'Oh my God, Tommy has no school friends! He's going to have trouble integrating with people for the rest of his life if we don't fix this now. We have to do something!' I was like a mad woman and I succeeded in convincing Hunter that it was the end of the world too, so after I hung up he called the pre-school straight away. Hunter is a problem solver as well, he's an executive vice president of a large international bank so he spends all day 'fixing' things, much like I do.

The pre-school was quite surprised to hear from him. It was, after all, only Tommy's first day, and it was to be expected that he may take a while to settle in because he started five days later than the other kids (we had been away on holiday). It was perfectly normal for the other kids to take a day or two to start interacting with him. Of course, in retrospect, I realise that should have been obvious to us and now we laugh about how we overreacted. But back then, trying to tell a lawyer and banker that some things in life don't actually need to be fixed took some convincing!

My husband is very involved in parenting, it's really 50/50 between us. I don't know how I'd cope if it wasn't. He is just wonderful. He's as busy with his career as I am with mine, but he still manages to run the household — he does most of the cleaning and tidying (he's constantly lamenting my penchant for making a mess). And he's incredibly efficient at his job so he works reasonable hours. My contribution to our domestic life is limited to the shopping, which takes me five minutes online. Thank God for the Internet!

It's interesting when you look at the way men in the corporate world deal with strong or vocal women. From what I've observed over the last 20 years, they seem to fall into two categories and it tends to reflect the role they play in their own families. The men who look for and value an equal partnership with their wives (whether working or not) are usually really supportive of the women they work with, and supportive of initiatives to keep women involved in their careers after they've had children. Mostly, they're all for a flexibility in the work environment because they know first-hand how difficult it is to juggle careers and kids. Then you have the men who fall into a more traditional category in terms of the relationships they have with their wives. Those kind of men generally have a more dominating approach, which also includes a genuine desire to take care of women, but in a more old-fashioned way. They often carry that attitude into their working lives.

I don't think that this has anything to do with age. You'll find plenty of young men who think that women are pretty accessories who need a man's guidance, and plenty of men in their fifties, sixties and seventies who think that is a load of rubbish and count women as their most valued colleagues.

I guess you have to remember that work is full of individuals who bring their personal beliefs into the workplace. People come with a lot of baggage, there's no denying that. And depending on what kind of baggage you're talking about, it could be a good or a bad thing.

marion
hume

marion hume

When British fashion journalist Marion Hume first swept into the offices of *Vogue* in 1997, the fashion industry was waiting with bated breath. Her arrival, preceded by the ousting of key long-time *Vogue* staffers, was one of the most anticipated fashion and publishing events of the decade. After holding posts at some of Britain's most prestigious broadsheets including the *Sunday Times, The Independent* and the *Financial Times*, Hume had developed a reputation as a tough critic and Australians were intrigued by what she would do with *Vogue*.

It wasn't long before she hit the headlines for casting a critical eye over the work of Australian fashion designers, judging them by the standards set by their international counterparts. Hume called it as she saw it, and if that meant proclaiming a designer's collection to be little more than derivative, then so be it. The industry was shocked. Unlike the worlds of film, art and theatre, the fashion industry had rarely come under such scrutiny before. Designers were up in arms. It was quite a furore over a few frocks.

Hume stood her ground and after being fired from *Vogue* chose to stay in Sydney and join *The Australian*, launching the newspaper's first ever fashion supplement and establishing her verdict of Australian Fashion Week as *the* essential judgement of the state of our local designers. Hume's rocky first years in Australia left her far from perturbed, in fact, on 16 May 2002, she became one of the nation's proudest new citizens.

My parents were quite radical for their time, in that they never really expected me to follow the traditional path of finishing school, getting a husband and then staying at home with the kids. I can't remember my mother or my father ever suggesting that, because I was a girl, I would have any less chance of doing what I wanted. That said, I didn't grow up in one of those kind of force-field homes where you sit around the dinner table and your parents tell you that you can be prime minister. They never asked, 'What do you want to be?' or suggested what I might be. The only thing that was expected of my sister Kate, my brother Al and I was that we would all do well in our own way.

My mother had a long career as a teacher. In fact, even though she retired years ago, the teaching shortage in the UK is such that she is back at work. When she trained, teaching was an incredibly respectable job. It still is, but I don't think people respect teachers the way they should, because our screwed-up culture teaches us to judge people's worth on how much they earn.

Having a working mum certainly wasn't radical when I was growing up in the late 1960s and 1970s, although it was unusual. I can't recall any of my friends' mums working. Yet there were still family expectations. We grew up in an English village, but my parents are from Scotland. My mum used to come home from a day in the classroom and cook not just dinner, but a three-course meal, which is what, as Scots, she and my father expected. While the meal was cooking, she would drive to the railway station to pick up my dad, who was on the seven o'clock train from London.

I think my brother and sister and I were lucky in that our parents really valued the arts, especially because they were both artists in their own right. I'm grateful for that, because at school the teachers tried to steer me away from an artistic path because I was quite academic. There isn't an art gallery my mother hasn't dragged me around. Even now, I'm hardly off the plane and she's like 'Have you seen the exhibition at the Tate Modern?' or 'Have you seen such and such a movie in Taiwanese about the trapeze artist dying of cancer?' My mother will go and see anything. My sister went to art school. I went to university. My brother's a craftsman in Los Angeles. We were allowed to do what we wanted.

I didn't start off loving fashion, or poring over the pages of *Vogue* as a teenager, I fell into it completely by accident. My mother has always been very stylish on a budget. My sister, Kate, is about the most elegant person alive. She just has this knack, which is hugely irritating especially as she also looks much younger than me and she's my big sister. I was Kate's kind of sidekick as a child. She was the one that was always doing ballet on the front lawn and going to drama school and getting involved in lots of different things, and I just trolled along. My sister was the one reading *Cosmopolitan.* I read novels. I was a very swotty girl. Kate went to fashion college and then got herself a job in London at Browns, which then and now is considered to be one of the most prestigious fashion stores in the world, owned by Joan Burstein and her husband — or Mrs B and Mr Sidney, as they're known.

I was very industrious, working on Saturdays in a store on Oxford Street in London when I was 15. Because I was so tall (I was already over six foot), I pretended I was 16. Then, when I was 17, Browns needed a Saturday girl. In those days, they had these things called incentives which meant if you sold the clothes they had difficulty shifting, you got all this extra money. The last time I bumped into Mr Sidney, he was still going on about all the money he had to pay me. It was the late 1970s, the era of Norma Kamali and the dawn of American fashion in London. Kamali's rara skirts were the thing. I was just flogging them out the door, selling them as fast as they could put them on the hangers. I loved it. I could sell anything. I could sell knicker-elastic if I had to.

I think that's why I've never been afraid to change paths in my career. Obviously I've been fired, several times, and I've been retrenched and I've worked for magazines which have closed from under me taking my pay cheques with them. But I've also left jobs through choice and without fear, because I know I can survive.

When I finished school I went on to university. I studied English Literature and helped start the first university paper. I thought the first issue was a bit dreary, so I put in a fashion page which other students thought was very low-grade. This was the time of Free Nelson Mandela, although he wasn't freed for a few more years, and as students we were supposed to be radical. I was. I have always been quite political and very concerned about human rights and I'm definitely a feminist, but I don't see why that rules out liking clothes.

I came out of university and moved to London. I won a young journalist competition held by *Honey* magazine, which was *the* fashion magazine everyone wanted and loved at that point. My story was about a night out in London. The prize was an electronic typewriter and a Filofax — not even a computer. I was thrilled. I'd learnt to type on one of those big old 'sit up and beg' typewriters. And having a Filofax in 1984 — I was just so proud of it. I loved it, I thought it was just the best thing.

There was definitely a culture of fashion journalism in England which began way before I started working. Fashion journalists were filing reports in 1947 when Dior unveiled the 'New Look'. I think it was much more critical then than it is now. When you look at the reviews of Yves Saint Laurent's early collections, they were savage. I think people forget that the women writing back then had extraordinary power. They may have worn hats and gloves, but they had great power within the newspapers, much more than their equivalents now, and they had very long careers.

When I came to Australia, I'd been a fashion journalist for years and I was completely unaware that this critical school of fashion journalism didn't really exist here. I remember Ray Chesterton writing something about me in the *Daily Telegraph*, about my being critical in order to stir up publicity and bring attention to myself. I read it, and it sounds incredibly disingenuous, but it hadn't even entered my head. I had no idea that the fashion reports I was writing for *Vogue* Australia would somehow be construed as an attempt to attract publicity to myself, or be seen as some kind of arrogant attack against Australian culture. I was just doing the same job I'd always done, writing an honest appraisal of what I saw.

I was really astonished by that controversy. I actually thought what I wrote was quite tame. I'd written show reports for American *Vogue* which were not particularly soft, so it's not like *Vogue* is never critical. I was just astonished that people saw it as some kind of highbrow, hypercritical assault on Australia's nationhood.

I've never been intimidated at work, not even in the early days when I first started working in newspapers. Maybe being six foot two gives you a completely different view of life. I've always thought that. I'm empowered to look at the bald spots that men do not admit they have, and they know that I know they're there. And I know who dyes their hair — I've seen their roots. Maybe that's why I've never really suffered any kind of sexism, and the one man who attempted it at work just seemed absolutely pathetic.

As for the glass ceiling, I know it exists. I've spent my career interviewing women for whom it has been very real, but I can't say it has been real for me. I've always felt I could climb as high as I wanted. Not that I haven't been exposed to another kind of sexism. When I was at the *Sunday Times* in London, the fashion page was known as the 'fluffy bunny' page, and they always wanted the girls with only just enough clothes on. There were times when I'd be called in to do things and get so offended because I was being treated like this sort of kitten. The next time I worked for News Corporation was here, at *The Australian.* It couldn't have been more different. I was treated as an intelligent person whose views were valued. *The Australian* was probably the happiest working experience I have had in my life. I had a two-year contract and then I stayed on another three months, then I chose to leave because it was time for both the fashion coverage to change and for me to move on. I have to say, it was the most pleasant leaving-of-a-job I have ever experienced, and I've had plenty of jobs.

I've never looked like a fashion editor. Even when I, all too briefly, had the figure for it, I was usually in Yohji. I kind of wish now I'd made more of it and gone to work in skintight pants and a boob tube! I think people expect fashion editors to be giggly and kittenish and coy. I've never been any of those things and couldn't be if I tried. Some of the men I have had to deal with might have been disappointed that I wasn't one of those girls. But on the flip side, my size has been a tremendous advantage. It completely disarms people. There are so many times that I've walked into a room where people were thinking, 'Oh, such and such a fashion girl is coming in …' and then I'd walk in and they wouldn't know what to make of me. There was a minute, when I was about 14, when I absolutely hated being tall, but it has been the greatest of gifts. Sure, I'd like to have a 25-inch waist, but if I had to choose between a great body or a tall body, I'd choose tall. It has given me my own unique perspective on the world.

Having been in the fashion business for as long as I have, I've seen how flirtatious behaviour and the power of clothes can be so useful. Especially in America, where I've worked on and off since 1994, I've watched people use their physicality and judge people by how they look. I'm not condemning it. It is fascinating to observe.

I don't think it's always been that way. Even Beatrice Miller, the grand editor of British *Vogue* when I first came into the fashion world, was very well put together but certainly not the head-to-toe-Gucci kind of woman you find in fashion these days. I remember how shocked we all were when Anna Wintour came to London to edit British *Vogue* before getting the top job in America. We were fascinated by her. To Brits then, she looked so perfect, while most of us didn't even brush our hair. We were astonished that she wasted so much time on being groomed. Now, pretty much everyone in fashion except me manages to look immaculate, but back then, the girls at British *Vogue* were in second-hand clothes with dog hairs all over them.

In the mid-1980s, I worked on a trade magazine called *Menswear* and then another called *Fashion Weekly*. It might not sound like the most glamorous start, but it was fantastic. I got sent all over the world on business trips. One day it was a trade fair in Cyprus, the next a swimwear fair in Jerusalem, then a weekend at a trade fair in Copenhagen. Now, I would be like, 'Er, no thanks', and even then, all of us hid under our desks when the trips to Dusseldorf came up, but back then I loved it.

If I'd started in national newspapers, there would have been a pecking order to get to go to Paris and Milan for the shows, but on these trade papers I just sort of held up my hand and they sent me. Of course I was in row 97 and even then I had stolen someone else's seat and, of course forged the show invites in the first place. We'd go to parties at Thierry Mugler's apartment or stay out all night at Les Bains Douches. It was just pre-supermodel era and the whole commerciality of fashion. It was much more free and I don't remember doing that much work. The other place I'd go was Spain. Barcelona was red-hot and as for Madrid, it was the time of La Movida, when people like (film director) Pedro Almodóvar and Antonio Banderas were just hanging out, and the brilliant designer Sybilla was doing shows, and Iman would be flown in to vamp it up on the catwalk.

I used to stay at the Madrid Ritz. I had this gigantic bed that was on a kind of raised dais and I remember thinking, 'Oh my God, this is so brilliant.' My limo driver was called Jesus! He looked like Javier Bardem and he was instructed to take me wherever I wanted to go. If there were no shows on, I'd say, 'Jesus, take me to Toledo!' and off we'd go sightseeing for the day. Once, I went to the island of Menorca for a trade fair where I only had to work for a day, but got to stay for a week. I met a man on the plane who had run Apple Records in the time of The Beatles and this other journalist and I just hung out with him in this island paradise.

I was completely obsessed with fashion then and, hard to believe now, but I had some incredible clothes. I gave away my Gallianos only when I moved to Australia and I just regret it so much. I actually used to wear high heels too, which is kind of peculiar to me now.

I first went to New York when I was 17 with about $7 and then I went back when my sister moved there in the early 1980s. I remember I phoned up Calvin Klein and said I was coming from England and I wanted to interview him. You couldn't do that now. I've got this fabulous interview, I spent five hours with him. By the next time I interviewed him, history had kind of been rewritten. Now fashion designers are like movie stars, you have to be vetted 1001 times by the publicists first and everyone, except Azzedine Alaia, is so careful about what they say. As for Azzedine, you ask for a glass of water and it gets filled to the brim with vodka, and then he starts on about how much he loves the Queen Mother.

I joined *W* magazine in about 1986, I think. Today, *W* is based in New York and it has a Paris office. But at that point, it used to be published in lots of different languages and its main European office was in England, where I worked, just down the street from the Manolo

Blahnik store. I went all over the world with *W*. Mostly I'd go by myself, sometimes with a photographer too. I just had this extraordinary confidence that I don't actually have now. Not only would I go anywhere, I'd think that I could speak the language. I remember when I was sent to Seville in Spain, the gap between what I thought I was saying and what in fact I was saying got me into some odd situations. Of course, every time I was misunderstood, I just said it again but louder. I think the fact that I've travelled so much over the years and met so many people is the reason why I can live so happily in Australia. I can live here very contentedly because I've done all that stuff. I think for some people involved in the fashion industry in Sydney, there is a sense that the world is passing them by, and in some ways it is. You've got to go out and see what's happening in the rest of the world, if only to make you realise what is really so fantastic about being here. I'm incredibly lucky. I've had these experiences that were so extraordinary that they were ridiculous. I've never done drugs, so it's not like those years were all lost in a druggie haze. I'm always suspicious of people who have had wild pasts, particularly pasts that involve enormous amounts of drugs and alcohol, and then they write memoirs. I think, well, God, I would have three glasses of champagne and I can't remember a damn thing about some of it, and yet they remember everything. Do they make it up?

I used to do the Haute Couture shows every January and July in Paris. In the last few years, that has become as pressured as the Ready-to-Wear, because it is all about big business. But when I started it was still huge fun and we'd have lots of time for tea at Angelina's on Rue de Rivoli. Now, there's hardly time to grab a baguette. When I first went to park my bottom on one of those little gilt chairs, I expected to loathe those rich women with nothing better to do than spend about $20,000 on a skirt, but it was so incredibly glamorous, that by the end of the first show I was just about willing to trade in my husband (although we weren't married yet) for a Bolivian tin baron who could buy me one of those gowns. I've got to know lots of those rich ladies and some of them are fabulous broads. I once travelled back to England with Mouna Al-Ayoub who has a diamond the size of a tennis ball on her finger. Mouna brought her butler along so he could serve us little snacks bought from Fauchon, which is the poshest deli on earth.

It was at the couture shows where I learnt to spot people's facial surgery. No matter how much a person denies it, I can still spot a face-lift although I usually pretend I haven't noticed. I've been looking at them for 15 years. The greatest fun I had was watching the changing faces in the front row. Actually, surgery has become rather more sophisticated, but as little as 10 years ago, you could see their faces literally disappearing under their hairlines.

I was always completely aware of what a privileged life I was living. In fact, one of the reasons I decided to take some time out was because I was becoming a bit blasé. I was getting to the point where I found myself checking into hotels and thinking, 'Oh, this shampoo is really not very good.' I've seen some very spoilt people, throwing fits because the fresh flowers that had been sent weren't gorgeous enough. I made a vow to myself that when I got to the point where I didn't want to behave like a six year old and jump up and down on the bed and get really excited at breakfast because the jam came in little pots, I'd give it up. And I did. I was starting to really hate travelling and I was turning into the kind of black-hearted old fashion hag that I'd vowed not to become. So I gave it up. Not forever, maybe, but certainly until I had taught myself to wake up and smell the roses.

I've met some great women in the fashion business. I've never really had a mentor as such, but I have some fabulous friends. One of my dearest friends is Kate Betts, who until last year was the editor of *Harper's Bazaar* in the States. She and I met when we were literally standing in the back row of the shows and grew up in fashion together. Alas, I grew out too, while she's still got very slim hips.

I know people accuse fashion of being superficial and on one level it is. Of course it is. But on another level, if you talk about clothes rather than specifically fashion,

I don't think we could be in a time where their relevance is more obvious. We all saw those tragic, horrible pictures of Afghani women in their blue burkas huddled in the street, having been completely robbed of their individuality, femininity and freedom by a repressive regime using the power of clothes. Then the minute Kabul fell, you had women on TV showing their faces. You could just see how liberated they felt. They were using the power of clothes in a different way. They were rejoicing.

Just before I came to Australia, I worked for the *Financial Times*, which is one of the world's most powerful, influential papers. What I wrote there — no holds barred as usual — could affect share prices. It was the time of the big fashion IPOs, when large fashion houses were being floated on the stock market, and I would just continue writing the way I did at the *Independent*, yet suddenly three per cent would fall off the Gucci stock. Not just because of me of course, but if I was critical, the people with the shares were reading it. I should say that Tom Ford always remained charming to me at cocktail parties.

Some of the big designers do take what you write about their collections personally and some of them let you know it. The Armani people called me at seven o'clock on a Sunday morning once to torture me about something I'd written. I criticised Chanel and was summoned to a face-off with Karl Lagerfeld, which was a nerve-racking experience. Valentino lets you know exactly what he thinks of you by what kind of seat you are given at his shows. If you wrote a good report about his collection last season, you're in the front row. If it was okay, but someone else's was better, you're in the second row. If you didn't write a thing, you're third row and if you've written something nasty, you have to ring twice for your ticket and you're in row 17. You know, they're Roman, they're emotional, they're passionate. But I've never been banned.

I remember coming face to face with one designer I'd written critically about. It was Hussein Chalayan, who has emerged as one of the most important designers. The fact that he does not dress Posh Spice means that he is not as well known perhaps as other designers of the same age. I think he's brilliant. But he did an early collection which was rather strange, which I wrote an article about. I was at a party with my friend Tamsin Blanchard, who is now at the *Observer* in London, soon after it went to print and she gestured towards this young, skinny boy and said, 'Have you met Hussein?' We'd never laid eyes on each other before, so it was like this electric shock went through us. He was obviously extremely upset by what I said about his work, and I felt hideous because he was so tender.

Those types of situations are difficult. It's really quite different to other areas of journalism. A film critic will view a creator's work in the dark, think about it and then leave. You rarely bump into the director. Whereas in fashion, the etiquette is that you go backstage right after the show and air kiss them. Even if you avoid that, you bump into them socially. It can be difficult — no matter how many millions some of these guys have in the bank these days, it is still their heart and their soul that they have laid bare before you and they are vulnerable to criticism just like we all are.

Compared to many fashion people, especially those who have been editors of *Vogue*, I have never been exactly showered with freebies, although I've given away a few Prada handbags in my time. My favourite gift ever came from Peter Morrissey after I asked in print who on earth would wear one of his designs. He had the exact piece I criticised made up in my size and sent it round. Not that I'm likely to wear an elephant-grey towelling mini-dress to a beach near you soon.

Whether they are giving criticism or praise, fashion journalists are central to the theatre of fashion. A fashion show is as much about the people in the front row worshipping at the altar as it is about the altar. You go to a fashion show and it's like an interactive experience where the people in the front rows are a part of it and they know it, which is why they have so many different pairs of shoes. I love that. I love seeing who's got what bag, even though I carry the same one, year in, year out.

The offer to come to Australia to edit *Vogue* came completely out of the blue. I think the word 'gobsmacked' would be appropriate. I'd spent five days in Sydney in my life, and I couldn't even fly out for an interview because I was finishing work on a TV documentary at the time.

My husband Pete was on his hands and knees in our London house finishing off an absolutely beautiful oak floor he'd spent weeks laying. I remember walking across it and saying, 'What do you think about moving to Australia then?' We'd literally just finished restoring our house. I was reading something the other day by an Englishman who had come here on holiday and decided the only Brits who ever move here are running from something, which is such rubbish. I had a contract with American *Vogue* which I loved. I was leaving the *Financial Times* to try and develop another TV documentary, we'd just finished the house and we were so not looking to move. But there was no way that I could say no. Saying yes was the most illogical thing I have ever done. But otherwise, I'd always have played part of my life on a split screen wondering 'What if?' So after a bit of toing-and-froing I said yes, and about a minute later Pete and I were on a plane.

Before I arrived in Australia, Condé Nast sent me to Paris to witness Joan Juliet Buck, who was then the editor in chief of French *Vogue*, at work. Actually, that was one of the most fun things of the whole *Vogue* experience. Joan is a very glamorous woman and she was living this dazzling life, existing it seemed on only extremely strong espresso and black chocolate served on a silver tray. Occasionally she'd take me to Dave (pronounced Da Vey) which is this rather ordinary-looking Chinese restaurant, which is legendary, and we would eat whatever Dave, the famous chef, felt like putting on our plates. Joan approaches life with such *joie de vivre*, she is reckless and fun and the atmosphere at the magazine just sizzled. I didn't know her very well then, but I'd watched her in the front row at the shows for years. Everyone else had these stony faces, no longer capable of expression, and there she'd be pulling faces when she hated the clothes and laughing with delight when she liked them.

I remember being in her office, which looked exactly how you think a *Vogue* office should look, and thinking, 'God! That's how you do it.' And of course, I came here and tried to do the same, but learnt very quickly that the Australian psychology is so different from the French.

My expectations of Australia were so wrong. But people's expectations of me were also wrong. There was an article published about me before I arrived which made me out to be some sort of fashion messiah. I didn't read it until I was on the plane and I thought, 'Oh my God, they're expecting a British version of Elle Macpherson to step out of this plane!'

I was under the impression that everywhere in Sydney

had a sea view. That sounds stupid, but I had been misled. The first time I came out for those five days was for Fashion Week, as a delegate for the *Financial Times*, I had my own driver. Everywhere we went — from Fox Studios to the Opera House — would somehow be via Bondi. Not knowing the geography of Sydney at the time, I actually believed that everything was on the sea. I now realise we just took the extremely long route so he could check the surf.

I didn't know much about Australia when I first arrived, although I'd seen a lot of Australian films. I'd seen things like *Sunday Too Far Away* and *Picnic at Hanging Rock*. I remember going alone to a cinema in north London to see *My Brilliant Career*. I'll never forget the first time I saw *Gallipoli*. The catch-line on the posters in London was 'From a place you've never heard of, comes a story you'll never forget' and I had never heard of it. After seeing the movie I remember walking up Regent Street with my sister absolutely sobbing. I still think it's one of the most moving films ever made. After living here, I realise that Gallipoli is absolutely central to the definition of what it is to be Australian so that catch-line on the posters must have been very offensive to Australians.

What Australia exports of itself culturally is quite different to the reality of living in Sydney. What I was aware of, seeing all the Australian films that came to London, was much more the kind of mythical Australia.

I was fascinated by it. All of those big expansive spaces and Aboriginal Australia was and still is fascinating to me. I guess I wasn't expecting what I found — a very sophisticated urban city by the sea. I think I was dramatically unprepared for Sydney and Sydney was probably dramatically unprepared for me.

Initially, I found Sydney society very perplexing. I couldn't decode it for quite a long time. I think the way that people do business here is very different and I found that complicated at first. Without going into it too much, I now know that what is considered acceptable is different in different cities. In the beginning, I was really confused by it. I was also very confused by the whole party nature of Sydney. I didn't realise that business and partying were very closely linked.

I realise now that some of the things we did at *Vogue* offended people. Like the shoot we did with Rachel Griffiths and the spiders, that seemed to attract so much hostile attention. Actually, the pictures were a lot tougher than the story I had in my head initially. The thing about fashion photography is that it is an alchemy: you might think of an idea and then you bring in the stylist, the model and the photographer, and they go out and they bring back their vision of your vision. Sometimes they bring back something that is so much better than what you had in your head and sometimes you go 'Oh'. When the famous 'Huntsman in my Handbag' story came in,

I remember thinking, 'Blimey, the Australian sense of humour really is sick', although the photographer was in fact American.

When I landed here, I think people thought I knew everything, which of course I didn't. And because of that, very few people on my staff were going to stand up to me. One person who did always challenge me was Kirstie Clements, who is the editor of *Vogue* now. She would march down the hall into my office and tell me exactly what she thought. When I was deep into my red earth fascination and thinking that everything should be shot in the outback — where I'd never been — Kirstie marched in and said, 'If we go out there, I'll be the one in the air-con with the Martini.' Now, having been to the outback, I admit that I would want to be in there with her! Kirstie and I are not close friends but we see each other and I hope we have respect for one another. I think she is doing a good job with *Vogue* now.

I think, back then, people built up this stern image of who I was probably because they didn't know me and I wasn't very available. I wasn't out on the social circuit much, so I guess people made up their own ideas about me. I remember Maggie Alderson spelling it out to me saying, 'You've got to remember that you're the new girl in school, and everyone's been waiting for you out in the playground, but you never come out to play.' But I was in that office with my sleeves rolled up.

Everyone knows that it came to a sorry end, but it was only a temporary sorry end. I remember having lunch with Campbell Reid, who was the editor of *The Australian* when I joined News Limited, and he made some comment along the lines of 'Wouldn't it have been better if you just came straight to us?' And I said, 'I wouldn't have missed that for the world.' And I still feel that.

I think every editor of a magazine enters the job with the awareness that it will end. These jobs are not the same as they were in the days of Sheila Scotter, who was the editor of *Vogue* for 10 years. Those days are over. Fashion magazines are a business and the business world is much more cut and thrust these days.

So it didn't end well for me, but I'm still glad I chose to unwrap this giftwrapped package that was Australia, even though the package turned out to be a jack-in-the-box that punched me on the nose. Ultimately, I'm still very grateful. Coming to Sydney changed my life.

I've had a lot of jobs which have been built into this jigsaw of my working life which, I think, is more interesting if fragmented. I would hate to have the kind of life, even if it were as the editor of *Vogue*, where I turned around at 60 and said, 'Well, I'm retiring, I've been in the same job for 30 years and thanks for the gold clock from Peter's of Kensington.' I knew that was never my destiny. I've always wanted to do lots of different things and live lots of different chapters in my business life, although in my private life I want things to stay constant.

The end of *Vogue* was very public and kind of humiliating. But the cliché 'What doesn't kill you, makes you stronger' is true when it comes to business. I don't think it is true for personal life where the scars are much deeper. Being fired by *Vogue* was so overshadowed by the bad behaviour of someone I loved and trusted at around the same time. I lost a job. Ultimately, so what? All the best people get fired. But being betrayed by a friend wounded me.

Dealing with everything was especially hard because I was so far from home. Sydney's home to me now, but it was more tenuous back then. I can't pretend I didn't feel hideous after I was fired, but I'm very fortunate to be married to a man who is incredibly supportive and I also have a very good secret friend here who I've known since I was 19, and who is just the most discreet and loyal person. When you are really down, I think you do turn to the people you've known for a long time. Those few months were difficult. Some people were nasty but when you come into a country as the editor of *Vogue* you are fêted and people feign friendship. I was never taken in by that.

Fashion can be an ugly business. I've been in it for enough years to have seen all sorts of things happen. I've seen people fall from grace. One of my best friends in the States is a leading publicist and she has her thing called

'The List'. That list is updated every 10 minutes and you are in or you are out. It's brutal. Pete used to say that when I did the shows I became 'Alternative Marion', this fashion person he just couldn't stand. But you do have to sort of strap your armour on to go out into that world. Your armour could be a fabulous Gucci pant suit in a size 8, or it could be a mental state.

I know that people made comments about how I looked and how I dressed. Certainly, they were upsetting, and occasionally things that were said about me in the papers were awful. I'd feel that I couldn't go out of the house, but it would only last for about 10 minutes and then I'd say to myself, 'Oh sod it, I'm going to go and have a swim.' I do not have a body like Gisele, but I made a decision early on that I could either spend my whole time wearing a kaftan or I could just get into my large-size swimsuit and enjoy myself. And of course there were designers who commented on the fact that I'm the size of a tank, in fact one of them even told my husband I shouldn't judge her clothes because I couldn't fit into them. That's ridiculous.

I have a real love affair with Sydney. I think it started like a holiday romance, when all you see are wonderful things. Then it became more of a relationship where certain things about the person you've fallen for are really irritating, but you stick with it and then it has the chance to become something deep. I think that's what I have with this city. I really, really love it. When I'm overseas and I see a picture of Sydney Harbour it makes me shiver, it is so astoundingly beautiful.

I remember having tea not long after I arrived with Caroline Baum, who is also from England. She told me it would take five years to really understand Australia. And now I know she's right. It takes a long time before you gain any kind of depth of understanding, before you can understand the nuances, and the humour. The breakthrough is when you find Roy and HG funny.

I've never measured success in financial terms. I think it's a very narrow definition. To me, success is to be able to go into your own head and to take the gifts that you've been given and do the best with them. It has nothing to do with selling stocks and shares and driving around in a Porsche. Although actually one of my dearest friends here has a Porsche and I quite enjoy going for drives.

You know when successful women complain and say, 'What I need is a wife'? Pete is definitely not my 'wife' but he is my support system. He has no hang-ups whatsoever about looking after the house. We don't share tasks equally, he does far, far more than I do. Perhaps in some relationships where the female partner is the bigger wage earner, it may affect the man's sense of masculinity, but he'd have to be a pretty fragile man, which is not Pete. He is way more creative than I am, but I happen to have been given a talent for which there is a ready market. In our relationship, sometimes it has been his time and sometimes it has been mine. Anyway, I know plenty of relationships where the woman earns more. It's not unusual any more.

Pete and I don't have one of those marriages where we wake up every morning and say, 'Oh, darling, I love you.' For a start, I'm a beast in the morning. We have spectacular rows. I think any honest relationship is going to have those moments. What is maybe unusual about us is that we've spent an enormous amount of time apart, months, while I was travelling. It is not true that absence makes the heart grow fonder. It makes things difficult. It is important to share life's experiences in a marriage, both the normal experiences of your day-to-day life and the really fantastic things. And if you spend too much time apart, like we have at certain stages, then you reach a point where you have to make the effort to be together. We want to be together. Pete isn't my best friend, I've got a couple of those. He's the love of my life.

He knows all about the fashion world. He was a designer, so he knows it inside out including the underbelly. He walks through the fashion world with a very large, sharp pin and punctures all those air-filled balloons. So I ban him from being anywhere close to fashion when I'm working. The only show he ever goes to is Akira Isogawa's, because they are friends completely separate from me. They share this visual language, so that when Akira's English wasn't as good as it is now, it didn't matter. I'd see them together doubled up laughing about something and think, 'Blimey, I didn't know Pete spoke Japanese.' But as for the rest of fashion, Pete's banned because sometimes I really want the fantasy. I want to see all those balloons looking all pretty and gorgeous. I don't want him to ruin it with his great big pin.

rachel perkins

rachel perkins

In the 1970s, when most young girls were playing with Barbie dolls and whiling away the hours in front of the television watching reruns of 'I Dream of Jeannie', Rachel Perkins was busy painting placards and attending public rallies to protest against racism and the dismal state of Aboriginal rights. At every demonstration Perkins stood alongside her father, the late Charles Perkins, a highly respected activist who played a key role in the fight for Aboriginal rights in Australia.

Not surprisingly, Perkins inherited her father's deeply personal passion for justice and equality and has emerged as one of the most prolific Indigenous voices of her generation. However, these days, you're more likely to find Perkins exploring and promoting Aboriginal issues from behind the camera rather than waving placards in front of it.

Perkins has worked in television since she was 18 years old and early in her career headed the Indigenous programming departments of both the SBS and ABC. Throughout her twenties, Perkins made many acclaimed documentaries including the 'Blood Brothers' series and in 1998 made her debut as a feature film director with the award-winning *Radiance*. In 2001, Perkins was back on the big screen with the critically acclaimed musical drama *One Night the Moon*.

She lives in-between Alice Springs and Sydney.

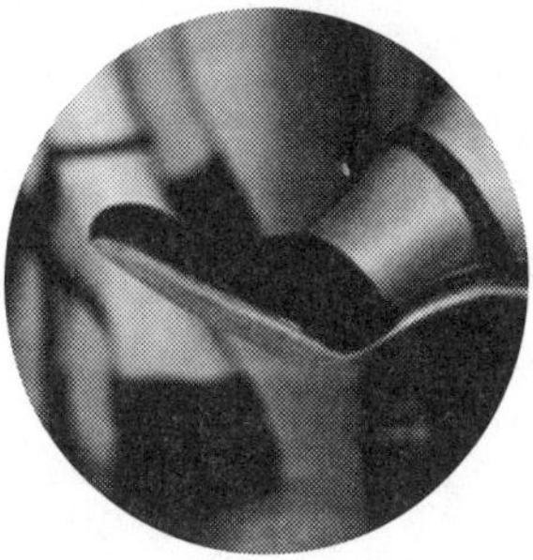

I always knew we were different, growing up in Canberra. There were only one or two other Aboriginal kids at my school and Canberra was such a white-bread town, it still is. We were always considered to be a little weird but we were accepted. The strength we got from our home life really helped. We were taught to accept ourselves and to try to use our difference as a motivation and something to be proud of. I suppose that's why I went back to Alice Springs, where my father came from, when I was 18. I was trying to come to terms with my Aboriginality, and make sense of all the things that made me different.

Most of Australia had little knowledge of Aboriginal culture when I was growing up. There was no such thing as Aboriginal Studies in schools. We really didn't have anything to identify with. I remember watching 'Rage' as a kid and a video clip of an Aboriginal band came on and I thought, 'God, there's something of ours.' It was the first time I'd seen anything like it on TV. The representations of Aboriginal people in the mainstream media were limited then, and they were either political or sporting — there was nothing a teenager or average person could latch onto. It has changed a bit now, but certainly Aboriginal culture didn't have a place in the world then, and it still doesn't much. I guess that's why I became a filmmaker, so I could put something back into the culture by making films Aboriginal people could identify with.

There was a subtle form of racism operating when I was growing up, much subtler than what my father lived with when he was young. He couldn't go to a swimming pool or a cinema as a kid. When we grew up the racism was different. We used to get called 'abos' at school and other things like that, so it wasn't all that terrible. I think of what my father went through and what his grandmother went through and I realise what we experienced was easy to cope with.

I think we all felt different, my sister Hetti and brother Adam and I, because we lived in two very different worlds. Outside our home there was never, ever any understanding of Aboriginal issues or Aboriginal history, or what was going on inside our household in terms of the political struggle my father was involved in. People just didn't engage with those things at all. Australian society was so different to how it is now. You would talk about land rights or language or Aboriginal spirituality and people had no idea what the hell you were on about. They just couldn't understand it and, for the most part, they weren't really interested. There wasn't any connection with the things that were important to us.

I think that's why a lot of people didn't really know why Dad was doing what he did, they didn't know what he was fighting for. Was he a politician? They either couldn't work it out or they weren't interested. I think that complacency or lack of interest came from the fact that many white Australians didn't really know Aboriginal people, they hadn't been to places like Central Australia so they weren't aware of the inequality of life Aboriginal people had. No wonder you couldn't engage them.

The friends I went to school with, who I'm still mates with, had no understanding of the world that I lived in outside of school, which is the same world I still live in when I'm not in Sydney. It really is a different world, politics and culture permeates your everyday life. When I came back from Alice Springs in my early twenties after living there for a couple of years and working for an Aboriginal community-based TV station, people would ask, 'What have you been up to?', like I was away on holidays or something. How could I begin to explain what I had been doing? People still don't understand that world.

Our family life was pretty normal when I was growing up. We lived in the suburbs. It wasn't a traditional Aboriginal upbringing, we didn't speak our Arrernte language at home and we didn't practise the traditional culture. It was more that our family was engaged in the politics of Aboriginality. Because of where we lived, we were quite distant from the culture itself. Our house was very politically charged all the time. When the news came on each night we all had to shut up and watch, and every political issue on the agenda was part of our nightly conversation.

There were always political demos going on and Mum, Hetti, Adam and I were always involved. I started going to demos since before I can even remember. The tent embassy and every major demo that happened, we were there. We were part of the planning: painting the placards, doing the T-shirts, all that stuff. It was a really dynamic childhood. Our house was always full of people, all the black leaders, people who were working in government. It was a very strong community to be a part of, but it was also very tense a lot of the time because the pressure was extreme. That pressure was just part of our lives. We certainly all knew what Dad was doing was really important and everything else had to come after that.

A few years ago Dad and I were interviewed for one of the *Good Weekend*'s 'Two of Us' articles. I was re-reading it recently and Dad talked about his one big regret in life, which was that he felt he'd never given enough of himself to his family and wasn't present enough in our lives. It's strange because I've never felt that. We spent so much time together, we were always with him. We understood that what he was doing was very important and he always involved us in it. And Mum was always there, we always spent a lot of time together as a family.

I moved back to Alice Springs from Sydney after my father passed away in 2000. I was there with my friend Aaron Pederson a while ago when an Aboriginal mate of his was thrown out of a bar onto the street, literally on his head. It was so aggressive that Aaron's friend had virtually his whole forehead scratched off. Aaron got really angry and it wasn't long before the police turned up but they arrested Aaron, not the bouncers who'd just injured his mate. I had to go and bail him out of the local gaol and write him a reference. The whole situation was almost an exact repeat of a story Mum told me about the first time she went to Alice Springs with Dad more than 30 years ago. It made me realise just how little things have actually changed.

Mum and Dad had just met. Mum was born in South Australia and is of German descent, so she'd never been to that part of the country before. Dad planned to meet his brother at the pub for a drink (he never drank alcohol, just Coca-Cola), but when they got there the publican refused to serve them because they were Aboriginal. Dad got really angry, so the police were called and they arrested him, and Mum had to go and bail him out of gaol. That was the moment when Mum understood that theirs was going to be a different life. Things were not as they seemed, Aboriginal people weren't considered equal. I think that set the tone for the fight she would endure with Dad for the most part of her life. She knew then what she was in for, she saw the injustice of it, maybe for the first time. She was swept away with the total inequality of it all and how terrible it was, and how important it was to change it.

She's still like that. When Mum was living in Alice Springs last year — she and Adam moved back there with me for a while after Dad passed away — John Howard came to town. As soon as she heard he was coming Mum said, 'Right, we've got to do something. You kids have got to do something about this. You have to protest. He can't just rock up in Alice Springs and get away with it. You've got to have a demo.' We were like 'Oh, Mum, we don't want to, we're so busy.' But she insisted, so we sat down and did the placards just as we had as kids and got everyone together. We organised this big demo and it was great, we got third-page national press, and TV and radio coverage, it was fantastic. Mum was so pleased. She is still very, very staunch.

Fighting for change is such a burden too, sometimes. I've realised in retrospect that it was a huge burden for Dad. He'd see something on TV or in the paper and he'd feel completely responsible for that particular injustice. He felt responsible for the Aboriginal race as a whole. Every day he would be thinking, 'There's a life at stake, we've got to do something, we've got to act. This is my purpose for being here. I've got to do this.' He lived with that daily burden, trying to change the world for Aboriginal people. It was an incredibly motivating force in his life but it also meant that he could never really relax. He'd take a break with us occasionally when he took a couple of days off but then he was straight back into changing the world again.

People just don't live like that, most people anyway. He lived a very stressful life and worked very, very hard. The responsibility and pressures meant that stress was part of our family life a lot of the time, but it also enriched our lives immeasurably. We lived through some of the biggest changes in Australia's social history with Dad. He was the first Aboriginal to get a university degree, he exposed the institutionalised racism that ruled most of country Australia. He participated in the campaign that resulted in granting Aboriginal people citizenship, he was pivotal in the establishment of the Department of Aboriginal Affairs which gave our people a voice in government for the first time. The value of being part of such an extraordinary life can never be measured.

I think Dad's life was an amazing example of what can be achieved if you set your mind to it. An individual can make a difference and change things, and that's something worth aspiring to. Just knowing that it's possible is good. Knowing you should apply yourself rather than waste your life, flitting it away being comfortable. I think Hetti and Adam and I have all chosen to live our lives that way, to try and make a difference. Hetti is the curator of Aboriginal Art at the Art Gallery of New South Wales and Adam is in business. He worked with Dad a lot in his last years, they did a lot of consulting and project work to help economically advance Aboriginal people, things like negotiating better mining deals on behalf of individual communities.

Trying to further the development of Aboriginal issues is a big responsibility for all of my family to fulfil but I know I'm not the type of person who can just relax and go and design frocks or something. I really believe that you have to do something that contributes. It gives your life meaning too. It's a motivating force and you feel like you've got a purpose and direction.

We grew up with a very real knowledge of how things had been for Aboriginal people in the past. My sister was born before Aboriginal people could even vote — it wasn't until 1967 that we were granted this right. Although things have changed a lot and many things are a lot better now, it's easy for people to take those achievements for granted because they don't realise what other people had to go through to get us to this point. It's just like feminism, I suppose. Young women don't realise how much of a fight it was for feminists to create all of the equal opportunities they enjoy now without a second thought. I think it's the same with Aboriginal issues; but I was there to witness a lot of that hard work so I'm very conscious of just how precious those milestones are.

Witnessing such enormous change makes you realise that you are part of an ongoing chain of humanity; what you do in your life does affect things later on. I'm very aware of how important it is to keep that progression going. I think that's why my work has always been focused on Aboriginal issues; I definitely see media as a way of progressing that change or development.

I started in TV when I was 18. I wasn't attracted to TV as such, I didn't really know what I was going to do. I'd been living in Canberra and could have gone to uni and done Aboriginal Studies but at that time there wasn't a lot of work written by Aboriginal people. It was mostly white academics writing anthropological works, and I wasn't interested in regurgitating white theory on Aboriginal issues. I wanted to explore my own ancestral Aboriginality because there was a big hole in it for us. We may have been brought up in a hotbed of Aboriginal politics but we had little contact with our family's own Aboriginal community, mostly because we lived in Canberra. We didn't know what our dreamings were, we didn't know our language, we didn't connect with a lot of our relatives, we didn't even know a lot of our direct family very well. Here we were talking about Aboriginality, but it was a very politicised version of it. We didn't have much of a connection with the reality of our traditional Aboriginal heritage, so I decided to go back to Alice Springs.

Actually how I started in the industry was through Dad who told me about a traineeship that had come up at the Central Australian Aboriginal Media Association (CAAMA), which owned the Aboriginal community TV station Imparja. They were looking for a TV presenter for a current affairs show. Being a TV presenter was the last thing I wanted to do, but they were willing to fly me up to Alice Springs for the interview, so I went for it just to get the airfare up there, thinking I could stay for a while. I didn't get the TV presenter's job but they did offer me a job as a trainee in the TV department. That's how I started in filmmaking really, it wasn't intended at all, although I had seen some of the things CAAMA was doing and thought it was very exciting. The driving passion came later.

CAAMA had a big impact on me and a lot of other people that worked there, including other Indigenous filmmakers I'm still working with now. Part of our training was to do an Aboriginal Studies degree, and as part of the course we had to study native languages. Our boss, a wonderfully inspiring woman called Freda Glynn, would constantly remind us of our responsibility. Each weekly staff meeting she'd say, 'You've got a bloody role here. What you are doing here is not for yourself, you are here to be a conduit for your people. You are here to tell their stories.'

It was very motivating and we were all very aware that what we were doing was important. We were putting Aboriginal languages on TV for the first time, we were making TV which explored critical social issues. Alice Springs really is the coal face of black–white relations. It is a very politically charged place, politics permeates the town. That was the kind of environment we were working in and where I made my early film and video work. I think that's why I didn't make personal, exploratory type films, even though the subject of Aboriginality is obviously incredibly personal to me. I was determined to make films that said something and contributed in some way.

The first big documentary I did, 'Freedom Ride' about Dad, came out of my desire to counter the fact that the people I grew up with did not know that Australia was completely segregated up until 1967 by local council by-laws and Federal legislation. My friends at school just didn't know that. They didn't understand that a whole generation of Aboriginal people grew up being governed by such racist politics, and that institutionalised racism was still embedded in their heads. Making 'Freedom Ride' was about putting that history back into the public consciousness. It was also special to me because it was about Dad. It was a record of him.

Moving to Alice Springs was difficult initially. I was a trendy city type — I had purple hair and was into weird music. But CAAMA immediately opened up another world to me. We had to go out bush for weeks at a time to film ceremonies, to remote communities where people often didn't speak English. We'd film the old people talking about their dreamings and their culture. It was great to be able to have the conduit of TV to go straight into communities which still practised traditional Aboriginal culture and way of life. There are some ceremonies that are sacred (not for public view) but many of them are not. The Aboriginal communities were happy to be filmed for CAAMA, they saw it as an opportunity to document an important part of their culture, and took great pride in performing for us, knowing that many other people would eventually see their ceremonies. It was also a massive culture shock, but I was really ready to learn. I was only 18 so I was adaptable to going out bush and camping for months and not having showers. I loved learning how to track and hunt, how to make a fire, how to boil a billy the right way, how to understand the weather, all those bush skills. It was so much better than going to university. It was a different sort of uni.

Lots of things I saw on those trips really moved me. I

remember one six-week bush trip we went deep into Pitjantjatjara country near Maralinga in South Australia, where the British Government conducted nuclear bomb tests in the 1950s and 1960s. It's really a remote area and originally there were a lot of Aboriginal people living there but the fallout from the nuclear tests left many people suffering horrendously from radiation sickness. We went there to film previously restricted ceremonies. It was a very sad experience, the petrol sniffing was so chronic that all of the people in that area between the ages of around six to 25 had died from it. The entire community consisted of four or five-year-old kids and people over 25, and no one in between.

The elders who still knew their culture performed sacred ceremonies for us to film every night for six weeks so that a permanent record could be made, as they were concerned that they may not have a new generation to pass them on to.

It was so amazing to witness but also sad because of the context of the whole thing. It was strange not being able to communicate with anyone; I'd try to talk to people but they didn't understand me. I remember thinking, 'Here I am in Australia and there's this entire community that doesn't even speak English, isn't that amazing.' That particular trip was extraordinary in lots of ways.

I had many amazing experiences with CAAMA. Driving up through Arnhem Land, there were just so many. I remember being taught the right way to hold a goanna. I was flinging it around by the tail and this old man, Yami Lester's father actually, came up to me and said, 'Don't! Don't hold it like that. You have to hold it by the neck and the tail at the same time to show respect.' I was always learning. All of the people were very welcoming of me, even though I was a city girl who knew very little of her culture. The communities were so happy that someone like me wanted to learn more.

CAAMA created a window into traditional Aboriginal culture like nothing else before it. Mostly, the things we were filming — ceremonies and storytelling — had never been seen on TV. The whole idea behind CAAMA was to put Aboriginal programs on air to balance the huge amount of Western programming that was coming into communities via satellite TV for the first time. A community leader would either call us or we would approach them to film in their community, and the programming was very much directed by them.

It really wasn't until I left CAAMA in my early twenties that I started thinking about my own approach, about the kind of films I'd like to make. That was when I started doing my own work; before then my work was driven by the brief of the broadcaster or the communities we were working with.

My time with CAAMA in Alice Springs certainly helped me come to terms with all of the things I didn't know about my Aboriginality. The more I explore Aboriginal issues in my work, the more I understand things differently. When I first started working in film and TV, I thought only Aboriginal people should tell Aboriginal stories, but that's changed. I believe that collaboration is good and possible now.

The journey changes for me as I work through things in myself and come to understand things better — my motivations do change. When I first started, maintaining the language and culture and having it in the mainstream was most important to me. Then that graduated to a desire to educate and put back a history for people, and now I'm starting to think my work should be more about trying to get non-Indigenous Australians to somehow embrace Aboriginality as part of their own cultural heritage as Australians.

I want Australians to have more of a connection to Aboriginal culture, and a sense of belonging to it, so if you're born in Australia and you call yourself Australian, Aboriginal culture is somehow part of your identity. That's something we don't currently have in Australia, unlike in New Zealand where kids grow up learning about Maori culture and language at school, they know their land groups and the tribal groups. Maori culture is much more part of New Zealand's national identity than Aboriginal culture is part of Australia's.

It's nice when you get to a point in your work where you can also focus on the craft. I started out just trying to get the message out there and now I'm really much more engaged in the craft of filmmaking and trying to be really good at it. I'm still dedicated to portraying important issues and stories, but I want to do it better and more compellingly.

I was 21 when I left CAAMA and Alice Springs to work for SBS in Sydney in the early 1990s. I was employed as the executive producer of the SBS Aboriginal programming unit, which was bizarre seeing that I was so young. There weren't a lot of Aboriginal people in TV at that time and I was hired under unusual circumstances where SBS was trying to fast-track Aboriginals into positions of authority. I admit that I was given that job because of my Aboriginality, it wasn't because I was amazingly talented or anything. They wanted a Black person in there and I happened to be one of the few with any experience who was around at the time.

I didn't know anything about being a producer at all, I had no idea. I didn't know the first thing about budgeting or financing or staff management, or human resources. I used to sit in executive producers' meetings every Monday and everyone else in the room was about 58 and there I was, 21, trying to look the part in a suit, trying not to say the wrong thing, and not knowing what the hell anyone was talking about. It was a massive learning curve and really embarrassing most of the time. The staff at SBS were clearly surprised at how young I was, and I'm sure that some of them would have seen my appointment as a token gesture. However, having said that, there was never any open hostility towards me.

Aside from the awkwardness of it all, I learnt a lot there very quickly. SBS considered Aboriginal programming to be very important, they believed in it. They were very forward-thinking and it was a great environment to step into. TV was really changing at that time and SBS allowed me to do the thing I wanted most — to make good quality, adequately funded programming. It was also where I met Ned Lander, who I created the 'Blood Brothers' series with. It was the beginning of an intense creative and personal partnership I've shared with Ned for over 10 years.

By the time I got to the ABC, where I was hired to do the same job, I'd done a film school course in producing and had enough experience to know what I was doing. I had a really good boss for a while but then everything changed. Management changed and it became far less supportive of Indigenous staff. They wanted to reduce Aboriginal programming to a half hour slot each week, but I had other plans. I wanted to make an Aboriginal current affairs program, a sports program, a sitcom ... I wanted to do so much more than just half an hour of Black faces on TV once a week. We did make some good TV there but we never really achieved what we could have. Not long after that I left. I had to get out of there, every day was a fight and it was just too draining. That was when I set up my own production company, Blackfella Films.

I found the crossover from documentaries to feature films terrifying. I'd never had anything to do with drama before I made *Radiance.* Never directed drama, never worked with actors at all. They say you have to be really young to be stupid enough take on something like that without any experience. And I was — I was only 28. Luckily I had a really good cast to work with but I was still terrified. So many people had put a lot of money into that film.

Leading up to it was the scariest time, but once we started actually making the film it was okay. The cast was also quite inexperienced and so was my director of photography, which actually worked for us rather than against us in the end, because we didn't have any great expectations of each other. We all just tried to do our best and work it out. I think it would have been much harder for me if I'd had a more experienced cast. I'm still quite terrified about working with actors but I have a bit more of a handle on it now.

While we were making *Radiance* we had no idea what people were going to think of it or whether it was any good or not. You just can't tell with film. Even when you cut the thing and you show it to a few other people, you just don't know. The first time we realised that *Radiance* was okay was when we showed it at the closing night of the Sydney Film Festival in 1998. It was a really terrifying moment, there were 3000 people in the State Theatre and it was the first public screening of the film. When the audience started laughing at the jokes, and I mean really laughing, and at the right times too, it was like, 'Oh God, they're getting it, they're going to like it! Thank God.' Then we won the best film prize that night at the festival.

That was amazing. It was so special to all of us because we made *Radiance* with a totally Aboriginal cast and the film was about Aboriginals just as normal people. People who love, people who keep secrets and people who hurt each other, rather than social or political problems. Having the cast on stage that night was wonderful. It felt like a real victory.

Making *One Night the Moon*, my next film three years later, was equally terrifying. Thank God it worked out. A lot of people didn't know what the hell it was when they first saw it. They'd say, 'My God, they're singing. What?', which was exactly what we were terrified of. That's why we put a song at the very beginning, to let people know it was a musical. Get used to it, everyone, because it is going to happen again! The musical genre was definitely unknown territory to me then, I didn't quite know where we were going with it. We just made up the rules as we went along and tried to work out the best way of doing things. I think the fact that we were working with a real family — Paul Kelly, Kaarin Fairfax and their daughter Memphis — made things a lot easier for me, in terms of making the emotions seem real. It was difficult for Kaarin though, who had to imagine her own child gone, dead. Trying to put herself into that space was very hard.

The fantastic thing about making *One Night the Moon* was that it was so collaborative. It was wonderful sitting around a table with people like Paul Kelly and Kev Carmody (composer), Mairead Hannan (musical director) and John Romeril (writer) trying to work things out. 'Is that the best way? But then that will happen?' It was also very intense and there was a lot of hot debate, especially over the ending, but I won out in the end. Most of the team thought that what I did was wrong (the ending was actually Louis Nowra's idea — he wrote the screenplay for *Radiance*) and that I'd really fucked up the film. Then we won the gold AWGIE (awarded by the Australian Writers' Guild for screen, TV, stage and radio writing) and it was like, 'I was right.' Well, I wasn't, Louis was.

I think the courage just to jump into things like that comes from your upbringing. You've just got to get in there and have a go and try to do your best. If there's an opportunity, you've got to take it even if it frightens you. I'll always remember something Dad told me when I was trying to figure out what I should do. For a minute there I was contemplating doing an MBA in business. It was one of those moments when you think 'What am I doing with my life?' and invariably everyone suggests you get some 'real qualifications' and do a business degree. Dad said, 'Well, I don't know what you should do, but I do think you always have to take the hardest choice. Whatever your options are, take the hard one, challenge yourself.'

I did take the harder option then and I have ever since. As soon as I finish one thing I move on to the next hardest thing and then another again. It doesn't have to be something bigger, just something that is out of your comfort zone. There's a lot to be said for keeping out of your comfort zone and challenging yourself. The work stays interesting and it takes you on a bit of a personal journey as well. It's great to set yourself ambitious challenges.

Film and documentary making is such a difficult process that you really have to believe in it to keep going. It's so bloody hard to make these things, it takes so much time and effort, and blood, sweat and tears, that it's just not worth it if it doesn't mean anything to you. And it's such a competitive world. In Australia, a feature filmmaker is lucky if they get to do two or three films before their career is over.

I get offered different projects and I think, well, I could do this or that, but realistically I have to look at it as being three or four years worth of work.

Filmmaking requires a huge amount of thinking and processing to get things right. You have to find the heart of the story and work out the right way to tell it. That's actually not so hard. The difficult part is trying to manage all of the people involved. There are so many creative forces at play and trying to manage those people and their ideas, and the politics in any given situation, is always very complex. That is really challenging, but also part of what makes it so good. It's a gift to have the opportunity to tell people's stories.

After I made *One Night the Moon* I decided to take on a project for SBS. It was a big, difficult decision for me because it was a four-year project, a documentary series, which meant I wouldn't be able to make feature films for a long while. It is the biggest thing SBS has ever done — the first cultural and political history of Aboriginal people in Australia right from the beginning, even before settlement, through until now.

When the project first came to me I was a little hesitant because it was such a huge commitment. I talked it over with my brother, Adam, and he said, 'You have to do it. It's a really important series and it needs to be done in this country. It will be a great legacy and a fantastic contribution. You've got to do it.' I realised then how lucky I was to have the opportunity to do something of such magnitude.

My work has been incredibly fulfilling in lots of different ways. The connections I've made with people have been amazing. When you meet people like Harry Hall, who was in the 'Freedom Ride' documentary, you feel honoured. Harry was one of the people who stood outside the Walgett picture theatre in the 1960s and fought for the right to be allowed in. He still lives in Walgett. Going to the Torres Strait Islands and Broome and all these places where people really want to tell you their stories, being really open and generous with you. They are so grateful to be given a voice.

Dad's hard work had a lot to do with giving Aboriginal people a voice. When he passed away we all realised just how grateful people were for the things he achieved. It was a better experience than I imagine it would be for most people because we had virtually the whole nation mourning with us, acknowledging what a huge loss his passing was. Flowers were delivered to our house every 10 minutes the whole day of the funeral and for days after. The house was filled with flowers. Our mobile phones rang all day. We were buoyed by all of that support. Still, the sadness is with us every day.

It's really important for my family to keep on doing the work my father did. Last year I worked on the Yepperenye Festival in Alice Springs, which was the biggest festival of Indigenous culture in Australia. We based it on the Nuremberg rally — we wanted to create a nationalistic Aboriginal day. Aboriginal people state their nationhood with dance, so we had 40 dance groups there from around the country — the Torres Strait, Tasmania — they came from everywhere. They danced one after the other all day for 10 hours. We had 350 flags of each tribe on the oval. That night we had a concert that told the history of Aboriginal people from pre-contact up until today through song and film. We had 300 members of the stolen generation re-uniting on stage, crying and weeping and embracing each other. Even Gough Whitlam was there to have the sand poured back into his hands by Vincent Lingiari's son, just as Gough had offered his father a handful of earth in 1975 as a symbol of his commitment to the return of Aboriginal land.

That all happened in one day and 30,000 people came to Alice Springs for it. It was all in Arrernte country, which is my family's tribe. It was incredible for me on so many levels, as an Arrernte woman, and as one of the artistic directors. Everyone was just completely over-awed by it because it was such a huge statement of Aboriginality.

At the end of the night about 100 of us went back to this one hotel room and everybody started making speeches, one after the other, about their lives, how they felt about being there, what the day meant to them, how moved and proud they were. There was no drunken, fake bullshit. It was all really raw and tender and proud, an extraordinary moment. A lot of the people involved said the festival was the best event they'd ever worked on, and many of the Aboriginal people who came said it was the best thing they'd been to in their whole lives. It was completely affirming for them.

It's incredibly important for Aboriginal people to reclaim their culture and develop a strong sense of pride. It's part of the reconciliation process, but one that I think has been completely overlooked. Sometimes I wonder whether reconciliation is for Aboriginal people at all, it seems to be more about white people getting together to talk about their feelings. There never seems to be workshops for Aboriginal people to help them deal with all the hatred they've suffered and still feel.

I don't think many Aboriginals feel like they are 'Australian'. When people play sport for Australia it's hard for Aboriginal people to barrack for them. You don't feel like it's your country, you feel bitter towards it. You don't feel it's your flag and you don't feel part of the culture. When you go overseas, you don't say, 'I'm an Australian', you say, 'I'm Aboriginal.'

Most of all you feel bitter towards the flag and towards Australia's history. I think that's a huge thing Aboriginal people have to overcome. I don't know how it will happen though, because so few people acknowledge the depth and self-destructive power of these emotional and psychological scars. Maybe the arts can help that healing process.

Role models are also really important. Cathy Freeman's obvious pride for her culture is extremely important for Aboriginal people. She showed the world that she wasn't afraid of celebrating her Aboriginality when she carried the Aboriginal flag alongside the Australian flag. Those symbols are just incredibly important. In Alice Springs, for instance, on Anzac Hill there is a Northern Territory flag and an Australian flag. Fifty per cent of the town is Aboriginal but the local RSL owns Anzac Hill and refuses to fly an Aboriginal flag. It's such a simple gesture and it would make the local Aboriginal people feel so much more part of the community.

Moving back to Alice Springs since Dad passed away has been part of the healing process for me. Dad comes from Alice Springs, so by going back there I feel close to him. I have so many relatives up here, thousands of cousins. My dad's family was one of the biggest in Alice Springs. I can't remember who they all are, or all of their names. I think they're proud of Dad but Alice Springs is a funny town. People can be ungenerous in certain situations, but there is a lot of pride from people who did know Dad well. It's overwhelming. When they find out I'm Dad's daughter, some just break down and cry and embrace me.

I'm happy to be in Alice now. It's no longer the place it was when my father left, when an Aboriginal person couldn't walk on the pavement alongside a white person. We're the first generation who can truly sit up here and do whatever we want. This town is ours. I can't tell you how fantastic that is.

I'm learning my language again and I'm forming relationships with some of my relatives. I come back to Sydney a lot for meetings and filming, but I love coming back to Alice so I don't have to engage with any of that stuff for a while. I go bush and camp out a lot. To be able to live in both worlds is fantastic.

I came out of a long-term, very intense love and work relationship last year. It can be very demanding on a relationship to be so tied up in that stuff, but it's unavoidable I guess, because anyone I'm with has to have that political understanding. I'm pretty fiercely independent and my family is my 'rock' in lots of ways. I don't need someone in my life all the time. I'm so work orientated and I find that really fulfilling. It would be nice to find the right person, though, you know the fantasy, but we'll see.

Some people are surprised at how close my family is. I first moved out of home when I was 16 but moved back in with Mum, Dad and Hetti when I was 30. I still live with the family when I'm in Sydney and I enjoy it a lot. Everyone who comes into our lives, partners in particular, are always amazed at the amount of interaction between us. Having a relationship with one of us is like having a relationship with the whole family. That must be very hard sometimes, but it's part of the package. It's always pretty clear — if you want to go out with me, you go out with my family too, and that's that.

Friendship is really important to me as well. A lot of the people I work with are my really good friends; it's really essential to work with people you like and for me those relationships usually last for years and years. I've got a really big circle of friends and I like socialising and having them around all the time. Our house is always full of people. I like that a lot, and it's such a relief to be able to sit around and just enjoy myself. You can take yourself a bit too seriously sometimes.

I especially love my old school friends from Canberra and my Alice Springs friends because they're not in the industry. I'm just the person they grew up with. We don't talk about film, we don't even talk about work. We just talk about whatever friends talk about. I like that relief.

simone young

simone young

Every once in a while, a woman like Simone Young comes along who, unperturbed by the fact that the odds are stacked against her, goes on to rewrite the rules and become one of the great success stories in her field.

At 26 and already pregnant with her first child, Young headed to Europe with her husband, full of dreams of conducting the world's most prestigious opera and symphony orchestras. She found herself in a world heavily cloaked in tradition and one that had no place for women. Especially a young and foreign one.

Young turned that tradition on its head and became the first woman, and often the first Australian, to conduct many of the world's great orchestras.

In 2001, after living in Europe for more than a decade, Young returned to Australia to take up the post of music director of Opera Australia. In-between the Australian opera season, Young continues to conduct around the world.

I grew up watching the Opera House being built. We lived in Manly when I was a child and I'd travel to the city on the ferry for music lessons. As the ferry passed by the Opera House I'd dream of performing there but I never imagined for a moment that it would actually happen. Now, when my four year old sees the Opera House she points at it and says, 'That's Mummy's office.' It's quite surreal.

I hadn't spent more than a month or two here every couple of years until I took up my post at Opera Australia. I still only spend six months of the year in Australia at the moment because my family and I are based in England.

In 1986 my husband, Greg, and I left Australia to live in Germany. Initially we only planned to stay for a year. I had planned to study as I had some scholarship money, and Greg, who is a foreign languages teacher, was going to take jobs teaching English. We had a stint in Paris, four months in Cologne and a couple of months in London.

I did some work with the Cologne Opera while I was in Germany and they offered me a permanent position starting the following August, so we came back to Australia, packed up the house and moved back to Cologne. I was actually pregnant with my eldest daughter, Yvann, who is 14 now, at the time. I was quite young too, only 26. Moving overseas and dealing with being pregnant at the same time was very stressful. I never want to put myself through that kind of stress again.

Those first few years in Germany were terribly difficult. We went from a very comfortable lifestyle in Sydney, not earning much money but not needing a lot to have a good time, to living in Germany where even just keeping the house warm costs a fortune. We had to get used to living in much smaller places. Then there was the added stress of Greg and I working completely different hours: he was teaching during the day and I was working at the theatre at night. There were days when we never saw one another.

On top of all that we tried to cope with having a baby in a foreign environment. Even something as simple as finding a doctor or a hospital to give birth in required a herculean effort. Those practical, everyday things are so much more difficult to organise when you're in a new country. It's not just the language barrier but a whole new culture and physical environment you have to get used to. And hopefully, some day, feel some sense of belonging to. And then there was the added difficulty of having a baby so far away from my family. But saying that, we originally planned to stay for only two or maybe four years. That was 15 years ago.

We felt very much on the outside of it all when we first moved to Cologne. We were in love with the idea of living in Europe, otherwise we would never have made the move, but the reality was quite different to the dream. Those early years were a real struggle. There was just no support structure there — no grandparents, aunts or old friends to help out when you really needed them.

By the time I got to Germany I'd already established a musical career in Australia. I started conducting in 1985 when I was 24. It happened by chance. I was working as a rehearsal pianist for Opera Australia for a performance of *The Mikado* and then the operetta's conductor got sick so I had to fill in for him. I wouldn't have been given that chance if it weren't for the circumstances. I worked as a pianist when we first went to Europe. When I showed interest in conducting there people were a little incredulous at the idea. The world of classical music in

Europe is almost totally dominated by men, conducting especially. But I knew I could conduct. I've always had confidence in my ability.

I just watched, listened and observed as much as I could. I made sure I was 100 per cent prepared for every possible opportunity and just grabbed it when it did arrive. Trying to do that with a small baby, however, made life quite stressful.

Rising through the ranks of the music world wasn't easy. It was incredibly hard work but I knew I was capable. I had no idea what my limits were, I hadn't even started looking for them in my work in Australia. I just wanted to be challenged and Europe was certainly the place to do it. But having said that, the minute I got off the plane I already had three big strikes against me. I was a woman, I was young — which is a real handicap in a world where most conductors are over 50 — and I was a foreigner. From Australia of all places! On top of that I had a small baby in tow.

To get past all of that I knew I had to be supremely prepared. I have this firm belief that if you are thoroughly prepared, if you present yourself as the best candidate, not one of the good ones but the best candidate for anything, then sooner or later you are going to get a chance.

You know the saying, 'You should always dress for the job you want, not the job you have,' well, that was how I worked. I didn't do the work that was associated with the position I had, I did the work of the person two steps ahead of me on the musical ladder. Sooner or later I had a chance to show what I could do and people were really astonished. That's always my advice to young conductors — do the hard slog and an opportunity will present itself to you sooner or later and when it does, even if you just do it competently, someone will recognise it.

I think a lot of young conductors are interested in the myth of conducting. They see the glamorous side. They see you standing there under a spotlight governing the work of 200–300 people. They see you in the newspaper. But what they don't see is that I never sleep because there is always work waiting for me and that I haven't spent more than seven days in a row with my four-year-old daughter in the last three months. They don't see that sometimes I have to set the alarm clock for 5.00 a.m. instead of 6.00 a.m. so I've got an extra hour in the day to study. There are weeks on end where I only sleep three or four hours a night because there just aren't enough hours in the day to get everything done.

But if you don't put in the hard work, you're never going to be good at what you do or feel that you're giving your best. You can never be perfect in this business and none of us have unshatterable self-confidence. I know I come across as confident and I am confident about what

I'm capable of but artists are, by their very definition, so full of doubts about their ability.

I think that's because what we do is impossible to quantify. You can't say, 'Well, I raised sales by $2 million this year.' How can I prove I am conducting better this year than I did last year? And it's hard not to take things personally when people judge your work. It's difficult not to take a negative review as a personal judgement against you, because you are your work.

I think I'm good at handling challenges. Those first years in Germany taught me a lot about dealing with life. There were so many things going against me, but they were all things I was incapable of changing. Early on I realised that they just weren't worth worrying about. If anybody had a problem with my age, or the fact that I was a woman, it was their problem, not mine. I proved myself through my work.

Sure, I came across some idiots. Actually, there were plenty of them. When I was a house conductor at the Cologne Opera there was one guy in the orchestra who told me exactly what he thought of me. The company had this system where the orchestra got to vote on whether they wanted to continue working with each of the house conductors. The orchestra had that kind of power. Because I was a house conductor, eventually they were given the opportunity to vote on me. After the musicians voted, one of them, a man, came up to me and said,

'I think you should know that I voted against you, but it wasn't because of your music making. I really like what you do with the music. In fact you're better than most of the men we have here but I just don't think it's appropriate for an orchestra of this stature to be conducted by a woman.'

I was completely gobsmacked. Firstly, I couldn't believe that people still thought like that. It was the late 1980s, for God's sake, not the 1950s. And secondly, I couldn't understand why this man was compelled to actually tell me, and so self-righteously, no less. What did he expect me to say? 'Oh, you're right. Yes, well, I should just pack up and go home then.' What an idiot. I guess that kind of attitude was the reason why there were so few women in the music world in Europe when I arrived, especially conductors.

I made my debut as a conductor in Europe when I was 31, which is considered to be very young for a man or a woman. But archaic rules aimed at keeping women out of the upper ranks of music have existed in some houses until much more recently. A few years before Lucie, my second daughter, was born I was invited to conduct the Vienna Staatsoper, which is one of the most traditional orchestras in the world. The orchestra was made up entirely of men and all of them over 40. It was actually against their rules to employ female musicians. I found that mind boggling, I mean it was 1993. It was hard to believe that sexist rules like that actually still existed. They got a bit of a shock when I turned up. I was the first woman to ever conduct that orchestra.

The ban on employing female musicians lasted until early 1997. People started boycotting their concerts when they went on tour, especially in America, so I think they changed their minds more for financial reasons than anything else.

I was actually conducting them the day the 'yes' vote was announced. It was my first time conducting *Lohengrin*, which is a huge piece, four and a bit hours, and I was seven-and-a-half months pregnant. I was a woman all right and what was normally considered an incapacitated one at that. The irony was just a little bit in their face.

I was also the first woman to conduct the State Opera in Munich, the Paris Opera Bastille and the State Opera in Hamburg. I can read off a list of firsts, which is fun from a historical point of view but not all that interesting to me. What I'm most proud of is that I was the first Australian to conduct in many of these houses in the last 30 years, often the first Australian ever.

I think being a foreigner actually helped me, in the beginning especially. Had I been an Austrian or German woman I would have been expected to conform to tradition, and in the music world we're talking about a tradition which has no place for women in the upper ranks. Australia is far enough away from Europe to be planet Mars so they almost expect you to be a bit odd and not to conform to their society's norms.

Gender is much more of an issue in the music world when you're starting out. Being as good as a man isn't enough. To succeed you have to be better than the men of your generation. If you're only as good, then they'll just choose the bloke. It's as simple as that really. Once you get to a certain point, however, none of that matters any more. Once you've proved your ability the gender issue becomes irrelevant. I reached that point four or five years ago, thank goodness.

But I worked extra hard to get over that hurdle initially. I went out of my way to become fluent in German. Not being able to communicate confidently puts you at an immediate disadvantage; it gives people an excuse to dismiss or disregard you and I was determined not to let the language barrier become another strike against me. Learning to speak the language as well as my colleagues did was one of the few things I did have control over.

I speak German fluently now, to the extent that my German friends and colleagues say you couldn't pick me for a non-German. But, boy, I worked extremely hard at it. I spent a lot of time and money on learning to speak perfect German. There was many a summer when I went to language school instead of on holiday, and most nights

I'd come home after a hard day's slog at the theatre and spend the rest of the night studying and reading German newspapers. Once Greg and I split for six weeks and went to live with different families so we were forced to speak nothing but German. It sounds a little extreme and it was. We wouldn't do something like that now but that's how tunnel visioned you have to be if you want to succeed in a really tough field.

It would be the same for a man. People just think it's unusual for a woman to do something like that because we're not usually seen to be so single-minded and focused. We're meant to be the nurturers. We're not usually allowed to be that selfish.

By the time I had Lucie four years ago, things were much easier for me. My years of struggling were over but my workload was, and still is, consistently unrelenting. People look at Lucie and ask me how I do it, but it's actually a lot easier this time around. Mind you, I was back at work when she was 20 days old.

When I had Yvann I was at everybody else's beck and call, but now I'm the boss. If we were in rehearsals when Lucie needed to be fed, I'd just call a break. Even now when I'm conducting overseas there is always a room at my disposal for the kids and the nanny. I can do all of that now and I have the money to pay for a nanny around the clock. Conductors earn good money but I don't see much of it because I spend it flying my family around the globe to wherever I'm working. Lucie is already a gold frequent flier and she is only four!

Things have changed dramatically in Europe since I had Yvann in Germany 15 years ago. The economy has changed, the political situation has undergone a turnaround. When Yvann was born, West Germany had the lowest percentage of working mothers with children under five in the Western world. They also had the highest level, I have to add, of State-subsidised income support for mothers. The government was basically paying mothers to stay at home. It was a brilliant social system. Women could take the first six months off after the baby was born and be supported by the government. If you chose to stay at home after that, which everyone did, you could continue to receive non-means-tested support. The whole system was designed around the fact that mothers — note mothers, not parents — didn't work. But then the economy was rocking along so well that women didn't need to work and they chose not to. Society expected them to stay at home.

As a result there was no such thing as childcare for children under three, which made life very difficult for us. I couldn't afford to take three years off. The only reason I was in Europe was to work in music so there would be no point staying if I was going to be a stay-at-home mum. I just couldn't envisage that kind of life anyway — music career or no music career.

I was also the major earner between Greg and I, so I really had no choice but to go back to work. I was back at work when Yvann was only eight weeks old and Greg stayed at home to look after her. Leaving your baby to go to work was seen as some kind of sin by the Germans. It just wasn't accepted. People used to call me a 'Raben-Mutter'. Raben is the German word for raven or crow, a bird that gives its young to someone else to look after.

Greg was always the only father when he took Yvann to playgroups or to play at the sandpit. He would be harangued by the mothers, as if he was less of a man because he actually took on some of the responsibility of caring for his child. They didn't want to know him, they treated him like a pariah. Today the economic situation in Germany is completely different so you see a lot of dads pushing prams around in the middle of the day. It's amazing how fast it has all changed. Fifteen years ago a man playing in the sandpit with his three year old was something you just did not see.

I'm lucky that I'm married to an extraordinary man who has never had a problem with assuming that role. He really is extraordinary. I have to say that what he does is no more than what most wives do for successful men, but for a man to do it for a successful woman and not have a problem with it is still extremely rare. When we get invited to dinner parties he chuckles when his place card reads Greg Young — his surname is Condon. Actually he collects the Greg Young place cards, he thinks it's very funny. He is just an incredibly secure human being. I know I couldn't have had children and come as far as I have in my career without him. Certainly not without going a bit ga-ga. Actually I think I am a little bit ga-ga already, but that's okay.

It's still tough because I don't get to spend as much time with my girls as I'd like. That's really hard, but I'm very good at seeing the light at the end of the tunnel when we have a few uninterrupted months together each year in-between the Australian and European seasons.

When the girls were little I did everything I could not to let my work get in the way of being with them. I nursed them both until they were 24 months old, not a lot of mothers can say that. My youngest, Lucie, travelled around the world with me until she was three. We weren't apart for a single day or night.

Trying to do it all does cost you a lot emotionally, and physically too, and you do sacrifice many other things in your life. But it's worth the investment. My children make me a better person. If I'm a better person, I make better art. If I make better art I'm a happier person and that makes me a better mother. It's a cycle that involves all of us. I feel really angry that some women still have to make that choice between a family and a career while most men still don't. It's just assumed that they'll have both. I think it's really sad.

I'm really lucky that my kids are bright and healthy. They've been healthy from day one. My husband is healthy and I'm healthy — sturdy as an ox! That terrible cliché 'You have everything if you have your health' really is true. If we weren't, if one of the children were sickly, it would have been a very different story. That's when you just have to be there as a mother, as a parent, around the clock.

I think women are a little bit guilty of a conspiracy against fathers to a certain extent. We don't expect them to pull their weight and half the time we don't give them a chance to. I think we get a little protective of our territory. There are lots of family things Greg is better at than I am. He is great at planning the daily grind, what we are going to eat for dinner that night, making sure the girls have clean shirts to wear. I'm shocking at those things. I'm the kind of person who remembers to do the laundry at three o'clock in the morning.

Greg really loves music. He is a passionate listener. He always said he played piano long enough to know he should give it up. He's done some singing in choirs. He's what I would call an educated audience member. And of course now he's spent the last 15 years in Europe listening to the great musicians, the great orchestras, the great conductors and singers of the world. You name it, he's heard them live and probably met them.

I met Greg when I was teaching piano at Riverview, a boys' boarding school in Sydney. I remember I was only

19 at the time and I tried very hard to look older so the Year 12 students, who were only a couple of years younger, wouldn't flirt with me. Greg was the head of modern languages at the school. He was really interesting, very cute and he could cook! We would go to concerts together. I was shocked when I found out he was 11 years older than me and my attempt to look older was obviously working because he thought I was at least 25. Anyway, that was it for us. We've been married for 20 years now.

I was still studying music when we met. I was only teaching on a casual basis so I was out of work most of the time. I wasn't very interested in teaching, I only got into it because it was just about the only thing I could do. Greg always had great faith in me. He always knew I was going to do something special, even when I'd given up hope. There have been many times over the years when I thought I wasn't going to make it. There was a time when I couldn't even get work as a pianist.

When I was in my early twenties I'd see friends who were working in different industries earning mega money. I remember thinking, 'This is ridiculous. These guys have less than half my brains and I'm still struggling to make ends meet. What good is music going to do me?'

I had a diploma from the Conservatorium of Music but what use was that? There was virtually no work and what little there was, was appallingly paid. I couldn't do anything except play the piano and the flute so I thought, that's it, I'm out of here. I've got to change careers, I've got to get into something with a 'future'.

I don't know what came over me but I was quite serious about it. Thinking my professional music career was over (at 22!), I did an aptitude test for a data processing course. I passed the test and afterwards in the interview the guy who ran the course looked at my CV and said, 'You've trained to be a musician. Why do you want to do this?' I managed to convince him that, yes, deep down I really did love computers and wanted to develop a career in this 'exciting' industry.

He must have believed me because he told me there and then that I could start the course on Monday. That afternoon when I got home there was a message on my answering machine from Opera Australia. They needed a casual pianist to start next week and were wondering if I was available. Was I available! Needless to say, there was an empty seat in the data processing course on Monday morning. I find it amusing now that I came that close to leaving music for computers, of all things.

But there were more times like that, even after I had achieved a degree of success. I almost gave it all in again 10 years ago. I'd been in Europe for six years and I'd done quite well. I'd been a house conductor at the Cologne Opera and at the time I was working as an assistant to Daniel Barenboim at the Wagner Festival in Bayreuth. Daniel is considered to be one of the best conductors in the world and securing a gig with him is seen as a precursor to success. I was on the edge of really making it but the opportunity to take that next big step seemed to elude me. I remember I was in Paris rehearsing *Wozzeck*. He allowed me to conduct big chunks of rehearsals, which was a strong indication of what he thought of my ability. Even the orchestra loved me but the odd bit of assisting work, even if it was for a genius, just wasn't enough. Where were the job offers? All the praise in the world couldn't pay the bills and as a result of working so inconsistently we were broke.

I could see myself frittering my life away year after year with three or four performances here and there. Earlier that year I wrote to more than 12 agencies (who looked after freelance musicians and conductors) and I didn't get a single reply. I'm sure it was because I am a woman. I know a young man with the same CV would have at least received a reply.

Trying to sustain a life in Europe was becoming increasingly difficult, not just because of our financial situation. We missed our family, we could see our folks getting older in Sydney and we were sick of the cold and the wet and the greyness of Germany. We decided we wanted our old lives back.

Greg and I sat down and did our sums. We knew we couldn't afford to stay in Germany. And even if we could we didn't fancy the idea of spending another 30 years there if I wasn't working in music. So we decided to come home while we were both still young enough to rebuild our lives.

I thought it was best that I be realistic and try to do something else with my life while I was still young enough. I was thinking about working as a teacher or doing a Law degree, just something completely different from music. I was trying to think laterally. I think women are very realistic about their career prospects and when they see things are not working, they'll say, 'Okay, it's been well worth trying but it's time to move on.'

About a month after Greg and I made our decision to move back to Australia I told Daniel Barenboim of our plans. I remember saying to him: 'We've stuck it out for six years and things aren't really developing the way I'd like. I love working with you and I'll come back to work with you any time but I can't continue working for myself if we're going to be realistic. It's time to pack our bags and go home. At least we can say we've given it a good try.'

Daniel sent his general manager to see me conduct *The Abduction from the Seraglio.* He loved it and a few months later he offered me a gig. It was the break I'd been waiting years for. After that everything finally started happening for me so we decided to stick it out in Europe for a bit longer. (And we're still there!)

Not long after that I made my debut with the Berlin Staatsoper and the Vienna Volksoper. The following year I debuted in Paris with the Paris Opera and in Vienna with the Staatsoper and a year later I did my first gig with the Royal Opera in Covent Garden. A year after that was my first performance in Munich and a year after that was my first in New York with the Metropolitan Opera.

I think success often happens that way. The moment you quit wanting something so much is usually when it finally comes to you. When you say, 'Okay, this is it. I've given it my best shot. It's time to rethink,' a door suddenly swings open somewhere.

I'm very happy to be back in Australia after being away for so long. The beauty of coming from this place is the sense of ownership the public has of you. Even if you leave Australia in your twenties and never come back, Australia still considers you one of its own. Sometimes when I'm conducting here I'm moved to tears by the welcome I get from the audience when I walk into the pit. I don't ever want that to go sour.

I think Australians love an underdog and that's usually the position of any Australian trying to establish a career in a different country. I don't come from a musical background, I didn't have everything presented to me on a platter so to a degree, I've always been an underdog. I had to work incredibly hard to get to this point and Australians appreciate that. I love the fact that the Australian public is so incredibly proud of me. Being embraced by my own country gives me a feeling that is impossible to describe. It's a wonderful gift to have been blessed with.

After all this time I still find my work challenging and I'm glad of that. The day making music becomes easy for me is the day I hang up the stick and try something else. You've got to keep pushing yourself through boundaries to keep growing and evolving as a human being. I don't think I'm in any danger of reaching that point though and that's actually one of the things I love about this business. I know I'll never get to a stage where I can say, 'Right, I can do it.' There's always something more to learn.

I could be working on an opera that I've done several times before elsewhere and then in rehearsal a new singer will colour one of the phrases in a particular way, like nothing I've seen or heard before, and it opens the song to me in a way I had never imagined. That happened to me recently. I said to the singer, 'Wow. We have to stop playing this now. I need to go away and think about it because what you have done with this has taken me on a whole different turn.' It is so exciting.

Those moments when it all comes together are what I live for. Just making music. The times when you're in the pit and the audience can't see you, only the orchestra and the singers can see the joy or the pain and suffering in your face as you move through the journey of the music. If you want to express the music correctly, you have to have the courage to show all of that, raw and revealing as it is. That's one of the reasons I prefer conducting opera to symphonic concerts, where you are on stage and everyone is there just to see you. With opera, the audience is focused on the singers and all the action taking place between them on stage, so the conductor becomes completely unimportant. You're simply a channel for the music and for communicating how it should sound.

I'm very expressive and very naked with my emotions when I am conducting so it's nice to keep that private sometimes. Of course the audience hears the result — the music — but the emotional exchange between myself and the musicians is still quite personal.

It doesn't happen very often, but every now and then you get into a performance where you can just completely release control. You become the music. I don't know how to explain it. It's incredibly rare. If it happens to you once or twice a year then you're doing really well, because usually there is five per cent of you that has to remain attached so you're ready to react if something goes wrong. It's mind boggling, a musical orgasm. It puts you on a completely different plane, sometimes just for 10 minutes or half an hour or, if you're lucky, for the whole night.

But even for the audience, music and opera are such visceral experiences. When you hear an amazing voice, not amplified, but a raw human voice singing at you, it is amazing. And then with the opera, the singer dressed in an astonishing costume which turns the experience into a visual event as well as an aural one. It's pretty heavy stuff. When you add to that the power of what an orchestra can do if it's conducted dynamically, you have very powerful visual, physical and emotional impact. Every person we get through that door falls in love with it.

Opera is like all great art. It deals with human fundamentals like love, death and power, how those three are intrinsically linked, how one often destroys the other. Opera explores things like disenchantment, betrayal, violence and hate. Even though it is a traditional art form, the basic narratives are timeless and new works do explore contemporary issues. Last year we did *The Young Kabbarli*, which explored Aboriginal issues and this year we do another new Australia opera about Lindy Chamberlain.

One of the glorious things about this career for me is that, at 41, I'm really only at the beginning. As a conductor I'm still considered a baby! In this world you earn your wings when you hit 50 and you don't become a maestro until you're 70 plus. Your career just stretches in front of you, which is quite rare for a woman. There are not many careers where a woman's value increases as she gets older.

Most people are surprised to hear that I come from a completely non-musical family. My grandmother played piano but that was it. I taught myself to play nursery rhymes on her piano when I was three or four.

I realise now that coming from a non-musical family was good for me because I spent my entire childhood and teenage years trying to explain to my parents why music is so wonderful. It was probably quite good training, seeing that now as a conductor I'm still explaining music to people.

I certainly had to sell my parents the idea of me becoming a musician. They expected me to go to university and study Law. Australian society was still pretty conservative in the 1960s and 1970s. I was born in 1961 and if you had brains, you didn't become an artist or a performer, you went to university to study Law or Medicine. My dad was a lawyer. I was on the school debating team and I was a star literature student so it was just expected that I would go into law. I kind of expected it myself.

But I was always involved in music. I remember sitting my HSC in-between rehearsals for yet another musical I was involved in. All through high school I was hired by different schools to play in their musicals or concerts because I was a good pianist and I could play the flute. I remember thinking university was going to be just like high school — study crammed with as much music as I could fit in, so I thought, well, why bother with law? Just concentrate on music and be done with it. So I did. I enrolled at the Conservatorium of Music.

I remember my parents being so disappointed by my decision. 'But we've wasted such a good education on you and now you want to be a musician! You're going to end up a penniless piano teacher taking lessons in the back room of the local convent, what a waste!' they'd say.

I ended up leaving home and supporting myself while I studied music. That was hard but once I got involved with Opera Australia a few years later my parents' attitude softened. For the first time they could see I had a future in music and by then I was already married. That's all parents want, they just want to know their kids are going to be okay. Now that I've lived through it, I can say that my parents' concerns were justified. A musician's life certainly is tough but if you push through those difficult times you get to live a life doing something you love. And that is extraordinary.

I know I could have chosen a much easier life in musical academia. I would have had a very nice, comfortable life in suburban Sydney, teaching piano at a couple of nice schools, raising kids, going to mothers' luncheons. Don't get me wrong, there's nothing I like better than being at home with the kids with a video and a pizza, that's my idea of a great night. I've dined at the world's greatest restaurants with some of the most famous people in the music world, but there's nothing I like more than a bit of 'normal life' at home with my husband and kids.

But a comfortable life in the suburbs without being constantly challenged would stifle me. That kind of life just wasn't made for me and I wasn't made for it. You do pay a price for wanting more than that. If you're determined to have it all — a career and a family — you have to accept that you will cut yourself short somewhere along the way. And usually that means that there won't be much time left for you. How do you justify going off to the gym for an hour when that's an extra hour you could spend with your kids or studying for tomorrow's rehearsal? The guilt is awful but you do get to the point where you realise that you need to take time out for your own physical and mental stability. Your family's wellbeing depends a lot on your wellbeing, so it's important to give yourself some time as well.

Sometimes I have really bad days where it all just seems too much, but I know those days will pass and the good days massively outweigh the bad ones. I'm a glass-half-full girl though, which helps. I get that from my dad. I can't imagine taking on a career like this if you weren't a glass-half-full type of person. There's a certain degree of optimism you need just to keep going, to carry you through the difficult times. Otherwise why would you put yourself through it, and so publicly?

Now that I'm a parent myself I understand why my parents tried to steer me away from music in the beginning. You just want your children to be happy, and if you think their choices aren't going to lead them to happiness, then you try to dissuade them and direct them towards a different path.

If either of my daughters said they wanted to be a musician, I'd be really pleased on the one hand, but I would probably be overly realistic on the other. If they weren't displaying exceptional talent and ability by the time they were finishing school then I would do everything in my power to dissuade them. Adequate talent is not enough, it's just too hard.

But having said that, I think you have to present children with all of the possibilities in life. The best gift you can give a child, either as a parent or a teacher, is the confidence to know that there is nothing they can't do if they really, really want to. What they choose to do is up to them but you should never rule out any possibilities.

acknowledgments

My deepest gratitude goes to the wonderful women whose stories are shared in this book: Marion Hume, Collette Dinnigan, Simone Young, Gale Edwards, Libbi Gorr, Lee Tulloch, Rachel Perkins, Donna Hay, Elizabeth Macgregor, Jan Chapman, Kirsty Sword Gusmao and Liz Broderick. Thank you for being honest, inspiring, entertaining and insightful.

Thank you to Alison Urquhart for taking a punt and to Kate Pollard for being clever and cool.

And a huge thanks to Bill Tikos for being tenacious, fearless and for believing. You are a star.